The
TORTURED MIND
THE MANY FACES OF MANIC DEPRESSION

THE ENCYCLOPEDIA OF PSYCHOLOGICAL DISORDERS

- **A World Upside Down and Backwards:**
  Reading and Learning Disorders

- **Conduct Unbecoming:**
  Hyperactivity, Attention Deficit, and Disruptive Behavior Disorders

- **Life Out of Focus:**
  Alzheimer's Disease and Related Disorders

- **Through a Glass Darkly:**
  The Psychological Effects of Marijuana and Hashish

- **Psychological Effects of Cocaine and Crack Addiction**

- **The Mental Effects of Heroin**

- **The Tortured Mind:**
  The Many Faces of Manic Depression

- **Anorexia Nervosa:**
  Starving for Attention

Senior Consulting Editor Carol C. Nadelson, M.D.
Consulting Editor Claire E. Reinburg

The
TORTURED MIND
THE MANY FACES OF MANIC DEPRESSION

Daniel E. Harmon

CHELSEA HOUSE PUBLISHERS
Philadelphia

The ENCYCLOPEDIA OF PSYCHOLOGICAL DISORDERS provides up-to-date information on the history of, causes and effects of, and treatment and therapies for problems affecting the human mind. The titles in this series are not intended to take the place of the professional advice of a psychiatrist or mental health care professional.

Chelsea House Publishers
Editor-in-Chief: Stephen Reginald
Managing Editor: James D. Gallagher
Production Manager: Pamela Loos
Art Director: Sara Davis
Picture Editor: Judy L. Hasday
Senior Production Editor: Lisa Chippendale

Staff for THE TORTURED MIND
Editorial Assistant: Anne Hill
Picture Researcher: Patricia Burns
Associate Art Director: Takeshi Takahashi
Designer / Cover Design: Brian Wible

Library of Congress Cataloging-in-Publication Data

Harmon, Dan.
The tortured mind : the many faces of manic depression / by Dan
Harmon: introduction by Carol C. Nadelson.
p. cm. — (The encyclopedia of psychological disorders)
Includes bibliographical references and index.
Summary: Studies the most common of mental syndromes and how it
can cause tension or problems at school, work, and home.
ISBN 0-7910-4900-0 (hc)
1. Manic depressive illness—Juvenile literature. [1. Manic
-depressive illness. 2. Mental illness.] I. Title. II. Series.
RC516.H38   1998   97-44058
                                                                CIP
                                                                 AC

CONTENTS

PSYCHOLOGICAL DISORDERS AND THEIR EFFECT

CAROL C. NADELSON, M.D.
PRESIDENT AND CHIEF EXECUTIVE OFFICER,
The American Psychiatric Press

There are a wide range of problems that are considered psychological disorders, including mental and emotional disorders, problems related to alcohol and drug abuse, and some diseases that cause both emotional and physical symptoms. Psychological disorders often begin in early childhood, but during adolescence we see a sharp increase in the number of people affected by these disorders. It has been estimated that about 20 percent of the U.S. population will have some form of mental disorder sometime during their lifetime. Some psychological disorders appear following severe stress or trauma. Others appear to occur more often in some families and may have a genetic or inherited component. Still other disorders do not seem to be connected to any cause we can yet identify. There has been a great deal of attention paid to learning about the causes and treatments of these disorders, and exciting new research has taught us a great deal in the last few decades.

The fact that many new and successful treatments are available makes it especially important that we reject old prejudices and outmoded ideas that consider mental disorders to be untreatable. If psychological problems are identified early, it is possible to prevent serious consequences. We should not keep these problems hidden or feel shame that we or a member of our family has a mental disorder. Some people believe that something they said or did caused a mental disorder. Some people think that these disorders are "only in your head" so that you could "snap out of it" if you made the effort. This type of thinking implies that a treatment is a matter of willpower or motivation. It is a terrible burden for someone who is suffering to be blamed for their misery, and often people with psychological disorders are not treated compassionately. We hope that the information in this book will teach you about various mental illnesses.

The problems covered in the volumes in the ENCYCLOPEDIA OF PSYCHOLOGICAL DISORDERS were selected because they are of particular importance to young adults, because they affect them directly or because they affect family and friends. There are individual volumes on reading disorders, attention deficit and disruptive behavior disorders, and dementia—all of these are related to our abilities to learn and integrate information from the world around us. There are books on drug abuse that provide useful information about the effects of these drugs and treatments that are available for those individuals who have drug problems. Some of the books concentrate on one of the most common mental disorders, depression. Others deal with eating disorders, which are dangerous illnesses that affect a large number of young adults, especially women.

Most of the public attention paid to these disorders arises from a particular incident involving a celebrity that awakens us to our own vulnerability to psychological problems. These incidents of celebrities or public figures revealing their own psychological problems can also enable us to think about what we can do to prevent and treat these types of problems.

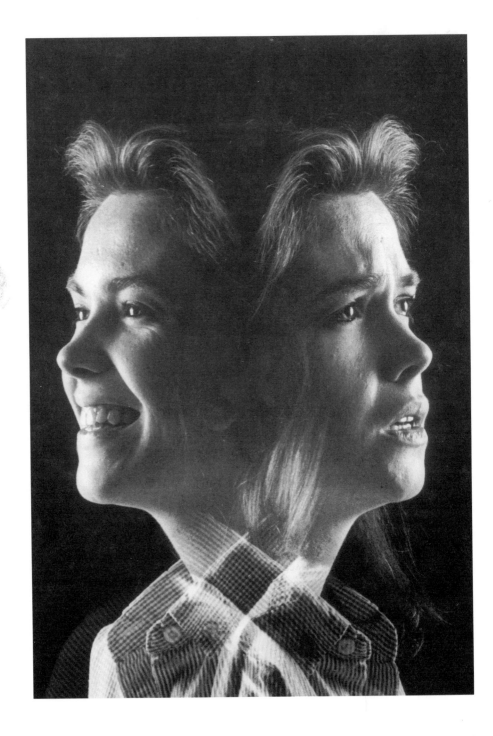

MANIC DEPRESSION: AN OVERVIEW

Perhaps you know someone whose mood often changes from high elation to deep depression within a brief period of time. It is possible this person is among the approximately 2 percent of the population that suffers from a psychological disorder known as bipolar disorder—more commonly called manic depression.

Manic depression is probably the most serious of a group of psychological problems called mood disorders. It can ruin people's lives. Some people with this affliction have become famous in spite of the disorder, like former actress Patty Duke, singer Axl Rose, and movie director Tim Burton. The brilliant Dutch painter Vincent Van Gogh suffered from manic depression, and this condition led to his suicide in 1890. However, someone you know could just as easily suffer from manic depression.

Often, the symptoms first appear when a person is in his or her teens. This can make accurate diagnosis difficult for a doctor or psychiatrist. And, as with many other psychological disorders, doctors do not fully understand what causes manic depression. In fact, its occurrence was rarely recognized until just over 100 years ago. But since that time we have learned a lot about how to successfully treat people with this disorder. Unfortunately—and alarmingly—doctors estimate that two-thirds of Americans who have mood disorders are not treated properly. The good news, however, is that with modern treatment people who suffer from manic depression can be helped.

This volume in the ENCYCLOPEDIA OF PSYCHOLOGICAL DISORDERS explains the history, causes, symptoms, and treatment of manic depression. It also defines and discusses several related mood disorders, such as unipolar disorder (depression) and hypomania. As doctors continue to study the causes of manic depression and research new methods of treating the disorder, the quality of life for manic depressives will only improve.

Dutch artist Vincent Van Gogh made this drawing in 1882. One of the greatest painters in history, Van Gogh suffered from manic depression nearly all his life. He created most of his works over a 29-month period, during which his mood swung from frenzied euphoria to deep despair. The mood disorder led Van Gogh to commit suicide in 1890.

1

A CONFUSION OF UPS AND DOWNS

Larry once was at the top of his profession. He had a Ph.D. in psychology and was hired by the Air Force to develop a computerized training system. He had a wonderful family. By any standard he was a success.

But Larry had a recurring problem. Radical shifts in mood hampered his work and caused stress at home. For a long time Larry was afraid to seek help. His job and home life began to fall apart. Ultimately, doctors determined Larry was suffering from manic depression.

Home for Larry now is a room maintained by a health care organization. "Work" for him is an ongoing project of translating license plates into a code of shapes and numbers that only he understands. He puts his work on post-cards. "Every image you see is infinity," he explains. "You can read into the card whatever is in your mind." He sometimes talks about spy plots.

Larry now lives one day at a time, no longer a man with hopes and dreams. Medication helps his condition but it can't restore the promising life he once had (Alger 1994).

■　　　　■　　　　■

Paulette suffers from manic and hypomanic episodes—roller-coaster rides of emotion. Here's how she describes one of her episodes:

> One night I woke up and started feeling good again. I felt I could do more with my time, that anything was possible. I felt alive and vital, full of energy. My senses seemed alive, colors were very bright, they hit me harder. Things appeared clear-cut, I noticed things I had never noticed before. There was a feeling of exhilaration, a sense of union with the whole world. (Jefferson 1995)

Unfortunately, when such episodes end, Paulette doesn't feel alive, full of energy, and exhilarated. She feels devastated.

■   ■   ■

L.G., a former executive, is enjoying his retirement years—or would be, except for manic depression. He started to experience mood changes when he was younger. They began to worsen after he entered his seventies.

During his typical manic depressive episodes, L.G. wakes up very early in the morning. He has trouble concentrating and remembering things. He has little energy. He even thinks about suicide.

L.G. is being treated both for his mood disorder and for other health problems. Disturbingly, his body seems to have become immune to certain medications that once helped him. His doctors have tried different prescriptions, sometimes in combination. At one time, after a medication had been discontinued because it had lost its effect, they tried it again—and this time, it seemed to help L.G. as before.

The roller-coaster ride for L.G., like many other manic depressive people, is not just ups and downs in mood, but also ups and downs in treatment. Whether the drug will work this time and lessen the severity of depression or mania is never certain.

■   ■   ■

Anna was a lawyer with a problem. Her problem was not a lack of clients or an inability to represent them well. Her problem was her inexplicable mood shifts.

These mood shifts made her, as clinical evaluators would say, "socially dysfunctional"—not a good way to be in a job that requires working with other people. Dozens of times during a period of ten years, she became delusional. At one point she thought a helicopter was following her. At another time she decided to wash a telephone by dousing it with water.

Anna lost her job through a series of incidents. Most seriously, she lied about how she was spending her time. Lawyers are paid by segments of their time. They charge clients for the number of hours or fractions of hours they spend working on a case. Some of Anna's clients and colleagues became suspicious of her time log. Had she really performed certain tasks she said she had? Or had it really taken her as long to do something as she said it had?

When the truth came out, Anna was given the choice of resigning or being fired. What a terrible way for an intelligent, capable professional

Depression is a major health concern. A study by the World Health Organization predicts that by the year 2020, depression will be the second most disabling health problem in the world, behind heart disease. Manic depression, or bipolar disorder, affects more than nine million adults in the United States.

to lose a job—because of a psychological illness beyond her control (Amaranth 1994).

■   ■   ■

Kay experienced radical mood changes as a teenager. While in her twenties, she began receiving lithium treatment for manic depression. A professional educator with a Ph.D., she was afraid to let anyone but relatives and close friends know about her illness.

For a while, she stopped taking her medication. She thought she no longer needed it and she was distressed by its side effects. The drug, administered too heavily at first, impaired her vision, making it hard for her to read. It made her feel clumsy and sometimes made her so sick she had to spend nights in the bathroom.

But without the medicine, Kay's problems multiplied. She went on unbridled, irrational shopping sprees, buying quantities of odd items such as snakebite kits. She later estimated that she had thrown away more than $30,000. Of her feelings, she said, "I could fly through star fields and slide along the rings of Saturn."

After these intense periods, her psychological pendulum would swing the other way, casting her into deep depression.

The question was probably not whether she eventually would attempt suicide, but when. When she finally made the attempt, her method was a heavy overdose of lithium—the drug that had been prescribed to help her. Fortunately, her brother rescued her, calling for help.

After fighting the illness for three decades, Kay—Dr. Kay Redfield Jamison, a widely respected psychologist, professor at Johns Hopkins University, Oxford fellow, and the coauthor of an important book on manic depression—"went public" in 1995. She wrote a book, *An Unquiet Mind*, the true story of her own ordeal with the disease. She is an inspiring example of a manic depressive who, with treatment, has learned to adapt while maintaining a highly successful career (Janis 1995; Toufexis 1995).

Many people fight repeated bouts of depression, a major health concern. In 1996 the World Health Organization conducted a study that projected that after heart disease, depression will be the most disabling health menace in the world by the year 2020 (Wartik 1997). A smaller number of people wrestle with periods of mania. During these periods, they seem to be high-strung and unpredictable. A still smaller percentage of people experience both types of disorder. These, the manic depressive, live in a particularly bizarre and troubled world. As the late rock and roll legend Jimi Hendrix once sang, "Manic depression is a frustrating mess."

THE EXTENT OF THE "MESS"

It is estimated that manic depression, commonly called bipolar disorder, affects between one-half percent and more than two percent of the population (An deBruyn 1994). More than nine million American adults (2.2 percent of people between the ages of 18 and 65) struggle with it, according to the National Manic Depressive/Depressive Association. By comparison, as much as 25 percent of the population may suffer from at least one period of clinical depression during a lifetime. Like other mental problems, manic depression is often misunderstood by both those who experience it and those who observe it. But its unwanted effects are obvious to all. In a 1992 survey, most respondents who personally knew someone with a mental problem said they would be willing to pay higher taxes to support finding a cure (*HCP* 1993).

An interesting study in 1993 indicated that most of us know someone with a "brain-related disorder," which might include anything from

Manic depression is more than just a personality problem. "Mental illnesses are brain diseases," explained Dr. Steven Hyman, the director of the National Institute of Mental Health, in 1996. Most doctors agree that psychological disorders such as manic depression are treatable and manageable.

depression to substance abuse to anxiety attacks. But "only one person in four recognizes the brain as the focal point of those problems." One commentator on the study concluded, "The general public's knowledge of brain diseases trails far behind knowledge of cancer, respiratory diseases, infectious diseases, and diseases of the circulatory system. The public also attaches less importance to developing therapies and cures for brain disorders than for other major types of diseases" [*HCP* 1993].

Some people believe depression is merely "the blues." Depressed people, they think, bring about their own problems. "Just get over it," they admonish.

That simplistic advice is futile. Steven Hyman, director of the National Institute of Mental Health, pointed out in a 1996 *Dallas Morning News* article: "Mental illnesses are brain diseases. Based on biomedical research, there is absolutely no justification for separating out mental disorders from other serious brain disorders. They are brain diseases just as a stroke or a brain tumor is a brain disease." Like many others in the profession, he emphasizes that brain diseases are treatable and manageable.

Michael Faenza, president of the National Mental Health Association, laments public perception of the problem: "The world's history has been one of fear and misunderstanding and superstition around mental illnesses. There's still a lot of misunderstanding. About half the folks out there think that mental illnesses are problems that have to do with character and self-discipline."

Many famous people, including composer Robert Schumann (pictured here) and author Virginia Woolf, have suffered from manic depression.

CONFUSING SYMPTOMS

Manic depression is usually first noticed during a person's late teens. Sadness and guilt, or, at the opposite end of the spectrum, hyperactivity and dangerous risk-taking, are common symptoms. But the disease can also be manifested by physical symptoms. The signs aren't always easy to recognize or to identify correctly.

One reason for the confusion is the variety of ways different people handle their illness. The *Diagnostic and Statistical Manual of Mental Disorders, Fourth Edition (DSM-IV)* explains that people in different cultures have different ways of expressing the effects of the disease. For example:

- People in Mediterranean and Latino cultures are likely to attribute manic depressive symptoms to headaches or "a case of nerves."
- Asian manic depressives typically say they are simply tired or "imbalanced."
- Manic depressive people in the Middle East may attribute the signs to a heart problem.

- Some Native Americans, when depressed, describe themselves as "heartbroken."
- Some people accept manic depressive symptoms as "normal." But they are not normal. They are signs of an illness.

THE RESULTS OF MOOD DISORDERS

Researchers have considered whether certain mood disorders, notably depression, might have a strangely positive effect on the work of artists, authors, and other creative people. Can a depressed mood give a better understanding of what the artist or writer is trying to express when delving into dark subjects? Objective information is hard to find.

Affective diseases—those involving human emotions—certainly have many faces. Our emotions vary, and they can be expressed both positively and negatively. Sadness, for example, is natural and appropriate in some situations. Glee, on the other hand, is a very negative emotion if we express it in response to someone's unhappiness. As an article in the *American Journal of Psychiatry* points out, "affective illnesses themselves are not something to romanticize. They bring pain and suffering and in their most severe form tragedy and suicide. In short, these can be mortal illnesses, and those who suffer them deserve the best that modern medicine can provide" [*AJP* 1994].

Manic depression causes people to lose friends and jobs. It strains family relationships. In severe cases, the sufferers behave so wildly they hurt themselves or other people. And in the worst cases, manic depression can end in suicide.

It is estimated that 15 percent of clinically depressed people who go untreated commit suicide. Alarmingly, an estimated two-thirds of Americans who have mood disorders aren't treated properly.

Manic depression is believed to have afflicted such famous people in history as artist Vincent Van Gogh, composer Robert Schumann, and writer Virginia Woolf. Famous people today, like Dr. Jamison and actress Patty Duke, are telling their stories and making the public more aware of the illness and its devastating toll on people's lives.

This book will explore the roots of this disease, its history, its symptoms, and its effects on victims and on all of society. Finally, we will look at the way doctors today work to solve the problem of manic depression with a variety of treatment methods.

Until the second half of the 20th century, the conditions in mental hospitals, like this Ohio insane asylum, were appalling. Overcrowding and lack of effective treatment methods were the main problems.

2

MENTAL ILLNESS: A HISTORY

The study and treatment of psychological illnesses is very broad and complicated. Clinicians today probe the depths of the mind to determine the exact nature of a patient's problems and symptoms. Pinpointing the precise illness is necessary if they are to provide the most effective treatment.

In the past, society was not nearly as concerned about helping these individuals. The main goal was to prevent the mentally afflicted from hurting other people and other people's property. Society primarily tried to keep the mentally ill out of the way, and if they could be prevented from hurting themselves, that was good, too. The notion of actually helping them improve and lead normal, productive lives was not taken seriously for many centuries.

Our ancestors shouldn't be judged too harshly. They had very limited knowledge of mental processes. Medications were homemade, based on superstition, and often ineffective. There was little society could do to help those afflicted with manic depression or any other type of behavioral illness.

All mentally ill persons were thought to be much the same. It didn't matter whether the person was manic depressive, schizophrenic, or aggressive—those terms were unknown. They all were said to be "possessed by the Devil." For ages, the only forms of treatment were religious rituals staged to drive out the Devil, and threats of physical punishment. There were almost no medications. There were no organized efforts to solve the problems caused by mental illness (Thompson 1994).

This was the status of European society when the American colonies were established. Native Americans, meanwhile, tried to cure their afflicted with elaborate rituals performed by tribal shamans.

Eventually, a few disorders came to recognized as medical, not spiritual, problems. Doctors usually believed the causes were in the blood or the digestive system. Remedies, therefore, included deliberate purging of the digestive tract or bloodletting. Not only were these practices very unpleasant for the

In the medieval period, the mentally ill were believed to be "possessed by the devil." When treatment was attempted, it was usually based on superstition and therefore futile.

afflicted persons, but they also were futile.

During the 1700s, many people who were mentally ill were simply locked away. Families confined their troubled relatives in a room for extended periods, sometimes for most of their lives. Poorer individuals were jailed or found shelter in publicly funded almshouses. They received basic care, but living conditions typically were bad.

In many cases the poorest people weren't treated at all. Some were auctioned away and put to work, essentially as slaves. Even after hospitals and asylums began caring for mental patients in the 1700s, poor people rarely received help there.

INSTITUTIONAL CARE

During the 18th and 19th centuries, hospitals and asylums assumed the care of mentally ill patients. Quakers founded the first general hospital in America, the Pennsylvania Hospital, in 1752. It treated mental patients, but not very differently from other patients.

The first actual mental asylum in America opened in 1773 in Virginia. The word "asylum" means "shelter" or "refuge." One of the definitions in Webster's 10th Dictionary is "an institution for the care of the destitute or sick and especially the insane."

Many social workers today would argue that "shelter" and "care" are words too nice to use in describing some of the early asylums for mentally ill patients. Aggressive behavior simply wasn't tolerated. Problem patients, including those who today would be diagnosed as manic depressive, were secured in irons or straitjackets, canvas outfits that bound the arms tightly against the torso so the wearer could not move. Some had to sleep in cages. Certain caregivers regarded the most severely affected patients as savage animals. These individuals weren't really cared for by today's health care standards; they were merely restrained and fed.

It was almost half a century before America's second asylum was opened near Philadelphia by the Quakers. It was called the American Friends' Asylum. This asylum and certain others that followed soon after embraced the teaching of Englishman William Tuke in providing "moral treatment" for its patients. No chains were used, and violent patients were separated from others (Thompson 1994).

A champion of care for the mentally ill during the 19th century was Dorothea Dix. Appalled by the inhumane conditions of a Massachusetts jail in which mental patients were locked, she began in 1841 a 40-year mission to improve their lot. As a result, more than 30 hospitals for indigent patients with mental problems were built.

By the mid-1800s, many institutions were making commendable efforts to truly help their residents. Patients were treated compassionately. Dr. H. Richard Lamb, writing in *Hospital & Community Psychiatry*, described: "Treatment included three to four hours a day of a variety of leisure activities, social gatherings, educational and religious lectures, and manual labor. The expectation was that such activity would prevent morbid thoughts and reeducate patients for their expected return to their families and communities. Clinicians were optimistic that mental illness could be cured and that the mentally ill could live in society."

However, by today's standards the efforts of clinicians of past centuries were crude. Some psychiatrists and doctors seemed to believe

The Eastern Lunatic Asylum in Williamsburg, Virginia, founded in 1773, was the first mental hospital in the United States.

patients could be cured simply by being in an asylum. Asylums became grossly overcrowded, many of them housing several thousand patients at a time. Personal attention to patients was impossible, and for the most part, as Dr. Lamb noted, "By the end of the 19th century most of the state hospitals had become primarily custodial."

LIFE IN AN ASYLUM

Let's step inside one asylum of a hundred years ago and see what it was like. In 1994, a lengthy historical report about a 19th-century institution, the St. Louis County Insane Asylum (originally called the St. Louis City Insane Asylum), was published in *Hospital and Community Psychiatry*. The asylum was opened in 1869 and was designed to accommodate up to 150 patients at a time. By the turn of the century, 30 years later, it was crowded with more than 600 residents.

The St. Louis County Insane Asylum was a good facility for its day. Its administrators had a high-minded objective, as stated in their 1876 annual report:

> Treatment of insanity, as practiced here, consists of raising the physical health to the highest condition it is capable of obtaining, by plenty of good nutriment, sleep, fresh air, cleanliness, exercise, and suitable medication; in diverting the mind from its hallucinations and absorbing delusions by means of work, books, papers, music, dancing, billiards, croquette, etc.; in encouraging the patient to express his self-control, and in firmly, though gently, impressing upon him the necessity of submitting to a healthy discipline, and of accommodating himself to his environment. (Evenson et al. 1994)

The asylum staff operated in two shifts, day and night. At night, the patients were locked in their rooms. Their only caregivers until morning were night watchmen making the rounds. There were no trained nurses for the first 27 years of the asylum's existence. The night watchmen functioned much like today's trained aides. They made tea for the patients, gave them drinks of water, sat with them during late-night ordeals, and administered medication. But lack of training led to tragic consequences. One watchman gave increasing dosages of a sedative to calm certain patients during the night, and three deaths resulted.

Most medications were basic and not very effective against psychological illnesses. They included cod liver oil, the muscle stimulator ergot, and bromide of camphor. Asylum officials experimented with different colored lights as a possible treatment, apparently with little, if any, worthwhile effect.

Patients were engaged in both work, such as sewing, gardening, and laundry chores, and play. Activities included dances, to which volunteers from the community came and participated. With the invention of moving pictures, cinema shows became a popular diversion for asylum inmates.

The asylum population included many patients who, by today's considerations, would hardly have been candidates for confinement. Records illustrated the sad lot of women during those times. Below are some examples of female residents and the reasons they were committed to the asylum:

- One was a simple-minded widow. After her husband died, the guardian in the settlement of the case connived to take her inheritance and have her institutionalized.

- Another was married to an alcoholic who literally drank up all their money. Depressed, with seven children, she threatened to commit suicide. This threat was considered grounds for committing her to the asylum.

- One woman was arrested for not wearing a hat or shoes in public while lecturing a group of men.

- One had a quarrel with her husband. After she moved their furniture into storage, he had her committed.

A CLINICAL SHELL GAME

In the past, people with mood disorders or any other serious psychological problem were often sent from one place to another, never receiving proper treatment. After a long-term stay at a hospital or asylum with no improvement, a patient with few resources might be sent off to the poorhouse. At that point, the person's chances of receiving real help for the illness plummeted from slim to none.

As is illustrated in the women's cases above, asylums were often overcrowded with people who did not belong there. For example, sending a criminal to the state asylum rather than the state penitentiary was considered a form of reduced punishment. This was a common practice by some judges and state governors. Perhaps the criminals were treated more humanely in asylums than in prisons, but their presence made conditions even worse for asylum residents who suffered from actual psychological illnesses.

The system did little to solve the problem of psychological illnesses and their costly impacts on society. It wasn't until the early 20th century that patients with mild psychological disorders began to be separated from more radical and violent patients for treatment.

During the first half of the 20th century, clinicians focused on the concept of mental hygiene, or improving the environments they believed contributed to psychological problems. Various social services were instituted toward that end.

Some proponents of this concept believed mental disorders were hereditary. They proposed regulating marriages and restricting the immigration of mentally disturbed individuals. Thousands were sterilized, a practice critics compared to the atrocious policies of Nazi Germany (Thompson 1994).

Dorothea Dix (1802-1887) was a social reformer who advocated specialized treatment of the insane. Her work resulted in the construction of more than 30 government-run mental hospitals in the United States, Canada, and Europe.

THE SHIFT TOWARD COMMUNITY TREATMENT

During the past century there has been a move away from permanent hospitalization. Some manic depressives still have to be hospitalized for a period of time, but often they can find help at community health centers and doctors' offices, and can be treated as outpatients, meaning they don't have to be admitted to hospitals.

The shift away from long-term hospitalization stemmed from growing problems with patient overcrowding. At institutions where thousands of patients were packed into the wards, adequate care was impossible. In fact, critics believed hospitalization worsened conditions rather than improved them. "Institutionalism" was opposed. If patients weren't institutionalized—shut away from family and friends for weeks,

This 1868 woodcut depicting a ward in a New York asylum shows one of the major problems of early mental hospitals: overcrowding.

months, even years on end—perhaps they could improve and become productive citizens.

During the 1950s and '60s, the number of resident mental patients in public hospitals dropped steeply. Many patients began to obtain care at community mental health centers. In addition to treatment, they received various types of rehabilitation and social skills training. Professional caregivers began managing their cases.

Today, patients are given medication and other treatments that have been proven effective by years of well-documented research. Modern treatments include lithium, electroconvulsive therapy (ECT), and anti-depressant drugs.

Treatment for manic depression is not always effective, even today. But manic depressive individuals today have a far greater chance of leading productive, happy lives than those in the past.

MENTAL ILLNESS IN THE EYES OF THE LAW

While the issues of care and treatment have been debated for many years both within the medical profession and throughout society, the legal rights and responsibilities of the mentally ill also have been examined. Should a mentally ill person who has committed a crime be prosecuted and punished just like other criminals?

During the 1830s, Dr. Isaac Ray wrote *A Treatis on the Medical Jurisprudence of Insanity*. He embraced the established assumption that insane criminals are not responsible for their actions and thus should not be subject to normal legal procedures and punishments. However, his theory went further. The law, by that point in American history, demanded evidence that a defendant, if pleading insanity, did not know right from wrong. Ray contended that some patients were psychopathic: they knew right from wrong, but could not help doing things they knew were wrong. Their mental problems should make them unaccountable for their actions, Ray said.

Not surprisingly, Ray was criticized by everyone from judges to ministers to newspaper editors. The effect of his theory, they feared, would be to make the concepts of "crime" and "insanity" increasingly synonymous. Many worried that society would not be able to maintain a workable system of criminal justice under those restrictions. That debate continues today.

Early psychiatrists pointed out the difference between a person who is "criminally insane" and an "insane criminal." In the first instance, insanity is said to cause the criminal act; after recovering from insanity, a person could theoretically return to a normal life. In the second, insanity is not the cause of the criminal act; even if recovered from insanity, the individual still would be regarded as a criminal.

The *American Law Review* published a paper by Ray in 1869 entitled "Confinement of the Insane." In his paper, Ray discussed the legal issues involved in hospitalizing the insane against their wishes:

> In the first place, the law should put no hindrance in the way of the prompt use of those instrumentalities which are regarded as the most effectual in promoting the comfort and restoration of the patient. Secondly, it should spare all unnecessary exposure of private troubles and all unnecessary conflict with popular prejudices. Thirdly, it should protect individuals from wrongful imprisonment. It would be objection enough to any legal provision, that it failed to secure these objects, in the completest possible manner.

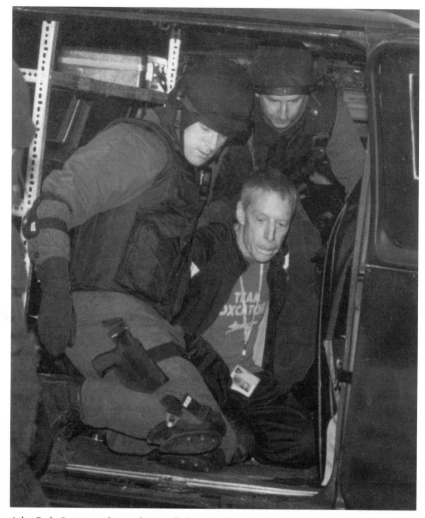

John E. du Pont was deemed mentally insane after shooting and killing Dave Schultz, a former Olympic wrestling champion, on du Pont's estate near Philadelphia in 1996.

One of the early famous cases of a murderer pleading insanity was that of Charles Guiteau, the assassin of President James A. Garfield in 1881. Guiteau's plea was rejected, though he exhibited clearly insane behavior. He was executed by hanging. There is evidence to indicate that his mental disorder may have been caused by syphilis, a sexually transmitted disease.

In general, the past half-century has been marked by a refining of issues related to insanity and the law. Mental disease has increasingly been viewed in much the same way as physical disease in the eyes of the American legal system. Lawyers have focused on patients' rights, such as the right to receive treatment, the right to refuse treatment, or the right to choose the kind of treatment received.

The actual impact of mental illness on the crime rate is also debated. Some studies indicate mentally ill people are not substantially more violent than well people. Evidence points to substance abuse as a more likely cause of violence than mood disorders. And clinicians argue that effective, community-centered treatment reduces the likelihood of repeated offenses by mentally ill persons convicted of crimes.

Other studies have shown that violence among the mentally ill may be several times more common than violence among other people. A connection between a crime and a suspect with a history of mental problems is usually deemed newsworthy. Some clinicians believe these connections are sensationalized. Comments one source, "When an ex–mental patient commits a crime, headline writers always notice" (Quen 1994).

When a person suffers from a mood disorder, other pertinent legal issues include the validity of documents such as wills and whether a patient's condition is grounds for divorce. "Mental capacity," when settling estate and divorce disputes, is a question that usually hinges on the circumstances of each case.

Another controversial question involves the family's right to order an affected relative to be committed for examination or treatment.

Bipolar disorder, in which a person's mood swings between manic and depressed states, is only one type of mood disorder. Unipolar disorder, or depression, is more common. Both bipolar disorder and unipolar disorder can be successfully treated.

3

UNDERSTANDING MOOD EPISODES

Mood disorders include both unipolar disorders and bipolar disorders. Manic depression is a type of mood disorder. Psychiatrists call this particular type a bipolar disorder. "Bi-" is a prefix meaning "two." Webster's defines "bipolar" as: "having or marked by two mutually repellent forces or diametrically opposed natures or views." The dictionary also provides another definition of "bipolar": "characterized by the alteration of manic and depressive states."

Similarly, "Uni-" is a prefix meaning "one." In psychiatry, unipolar disorders also are called depressive disorders. In this case, it means a person suffers from a kind of depression (such as major depressive disorder or dysthymic disorder) but not from manic problems.

There are two other types of mood disorders that are classified according to their etiology, or underlying causes. These two are mood disorder due to a general medical condition and substance-induced mood disorder. The first reflects the ways in which other ailments (for example, cancer or diabetes) can affect a person's moods. The second covers the various moods that might result from abuse of drugs or alcohol or from use or abuse of prescribed medication. Some of the symptoms resemble the symptoms of manic depression, and it often is hard for a clinician to determine exactly which form of disorder a patient is battling.

Now that we've seen the broad picture of mood disorders and the four main types, let's focus on bipolar disorders—manic depression. There are different forms of manic behavior and different forms of depression, meaning that there are different kinds of bipolar disorders.

Diagnosing and treating people with manic depression is a very complicated task that requires professional skills, experience, and ongoing study. In most instances the illness can be treated if the person will admit that there is a problem and seek help.

During his manic periods, the Dutch artist Van Gogh, shown here in a self-portrait, created most of his artwork. Van Gogh's work is probably the most recognized in the world, and his painting Sunflowers sold for $40.3 million in 1987. Ironically, Van Gogh was only able to sell one painting in his lifetime. He committed suicide in 1890 because of his mental illness.

Manic depressives don't experience the effects of their illness just once or twice during their lifetimes. Rather, the disease comes on as a series of "episodes," or struggles with the illness. Sometimes these episodes occur years apart.

According to the *DSM-IV*, bipolar disorders "involve the presence (or history) of manic episodes, mixed episodes, or hypomanic episodes, usually accompanied by the presence (or history) of major depressive episodes."

Below, we will examine the four different "mood episodes" involved in manic depression.

MANIC EPISODE

At first, some of the symptoms of a manic episode seem positive. For example, Erin, an outgoing, highly motivated, and self-confident young woman with boundless energy, manages a pet shop. She seems well-rested after only a few hours of sleep. But at times her motivation and self-confidence rise to abnormal extremes. During these times, less desirable symptoms also begin to appear. Erin becomes irritable, unpleasant to be with, and something seems wrong about her personality. During a manic episode, she believes she can see, hear, and smell more keenly than usual. On a sudden impulse, she calls up long-lost friends, or gives candy, and even money, to strangers.

She may strike up a conversation with a complete stranger in a restaurant and not stop talking. She might arrive at work very early in the morning and telephone her employees, who are still asleep at home. Self-deluded, she's likely to claim a personal friendship with the president of the United States, a famous actress, or a popular music group. She offers serious but meaningless advice about nuclear science, law, medicine, international politics, and other topics about which she really knows very little.

She becomes very irritated if things aren't done her way. Her conversation can turn angry and abusive. She tends to speak loudly, fast, and without stopping. Her speech seems "pressured," as psychiatrists describe it. Sentences may ramble from topic to topic and become incoherent. She is easily distracted.

In a frenzy of what counselors call "goal-directed" activity, Erin is liable to take unrealistic job risks. For example, she might start many new work projects, with no time to complete any of them properly.

Reckless driving and unaffordable shopping sprees are common. On impulse, Erin may buy expensive antiques or dozens of pairs of shoes. She often will indulge in expensive and harmful pleasures, not thinking of the cost. She initiates romantic affairs with strangers. Normally a

Mood disorders, like other psychological disorders, are considered "brain diseases" by doctors. Although scientists have spent hundreds of years studying the human brain, more research is needed so that doctors can better treat people with bipolar disorder, unipolar disorder, or other psychological problems.

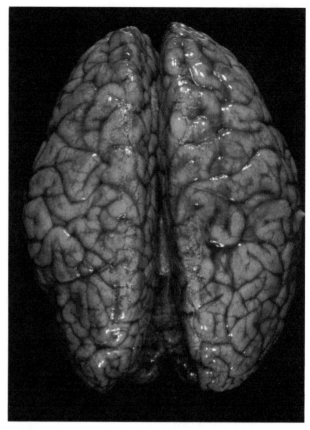

conservative dresser, she suddenly starts to wear gaudy clothes.

Mark, a student, exhibits behavior much like Erin's while undergoing a manic episode. He often misses classes and fails exams. He loses friends. He sometimes uses drugs or alcohol during a manic episode; this usually worsens the condition and makes it last longer.

Frequently, the behavior of people suffering from manic episodes, like Erin and Mark, becomes so outrageous that they have to be hospitalized. Otherwise, they may cause themselves serious financial or social harm. They may attack others verbally or physically, steal, or commit more serious offenses, apparently not understanding the difference between right and wrong.

Many individuals like Erin and Mark don't realize the seriousness of their condition and resist help while undergoing a manic episode. But after the episode is over, they probably will express sincere regret for their actions.

On average, people who suffer from manic episodes first experience them during their early twenties. These bouts are not uncommon among teenagers, however. And some people don't experience an episode until they are age 50 or older.

Most manic episodes start with little warning and develop quickly during a period of a few days. These wild binges last at least a week and sometimes as long as several months unless they are treated.

In at least half the cases studied, according to the *DSM-IV*, a manic episode occurs either right before or right after a major depressive episode (described below). Sometimes the person suffers brief spells of depression during a manic episode, but the depression usually lasts only a few moments or hours.

Certain types of medicine cause some people to behave in similar irrational ways. These instances are not really manic episodes. They are called substance-induced mood disorders with manic features.

Another similar but less radical ailment is attention deficit/hyperactivity disorder. People with this disorder, like those experiencing a manic episode, are conspicuous for their frenzied, impulsive activity and poor judgment. They, too, may deny they have a problem.

Unlike the manic episode, attention deficit/hyperactivity disorder usually begins in childhood. It is ongoing, not just flaring up occasionally.

HYPOMANIC EPISODE

Peter, a teenager who suffers from hypomanic episodes, displays many of the same symptoms as Erin and Mark. But his behavior is not as severe or harmful, and he doesn't require hospitalization. Still, his symptoms are alarming and can develop into a full manic episode. Fortunately, no more than 15 percent of people who suffer from hypomanic symptoms are likely to have a full manic episode.

Like Mark and Erin, Peter "feels good"—too good. He's cheerful, outgoing, and eager to socialize, sometimes with strangers. For several days, he feels either "elevated" or is irritable and easily excited about small things. He thinks he's a world beater. He is not so deluded that he thinks he's a rocket scientist, but he is overconfident.

Peter feels rested and ready to go after just a few hours of sleep. He's abnormally talkative and loud, frequently telling many jokes and making wisecracks, but he's not as hard to interrupt as Mark and Erin. He'll suddenly change the subject of a conversation for no apparent reason, and he's easily distracted.

Peter seems driven to accomplish things, and he's very creative. He surprises his parents by cleaning up his room without being nagged. He writes a letter to the editor of the local paper, and takes the initiative to do other things he's never done before.

But he is also overly impulsive. Like people who experience manic episodes, he might go on unreasonable spending sprees or start projects he never can complete. He plays hooky from school and neglects his studies. And while he's generally very cheerful during a hypomanic episode, he also can be antisocial and may use drugs.

To those who don't know them, people like Peter may seem to be just interesting, "hyper" individuals. But friends and family may realize something is wrong. They may wonder if the person could be under the influence of harmful stimulants. Even if this is the case, it may not be the underlying cause of their behavior, because the illness is not caused directly by drug abuse or prescribed medication.

A major difference between a hypomanic episode and the manic episode, described above, is that there are no delusions or hallucinations in the former. Counselors and psychiatrists who evaluate these people might not realize just by talking to them that their behavior is out of character. They may have to interview family members or close friends to get a true idea of how the troubled individuals usually talk and act.

It takes only a day or two for a hypomanic episode to develop. It can last for weeks, even months. A hypomanic episode often occurs just before or after a major depressive episode.

MAJOR DEPRESSIVE EPISODE

Manic depression is like a psychological pendulum swing. On one side, the mood swings unnaturally up and a manic or hypomanic episode results. At the other side of the swing is depression.

A major depressive episode lasts two weeks to six months—perhaps longer, if untreated. During this time, the person feels depressed and may lose interest in just about everything. There is little enjoyment in life, even in a favorite hobby. "I don't care anymore," may be the attitude.

In most cases, a major depressive episode develops gradually. It might begin with mild depression for a few days, weeks, or months before the more serious disorder takes effect.

A major depressive episode, lasting between two weeks and six months, is marked by insomnia, loss of appetite, nervousness, loss of concentration and energy, and feelings of uselessness or guilt.

A young person who has this problem may show it not so much by sadness as by being very difficult to get along with. A small child may fear being separated from parents to an excessive degree. Young or old, the person may feel unusually afraid or may cry over minor hurts. This person may worry too much or brood over things beyond his or her

The mood swings associated with manic depression can lead to drug or alcohol abuse, which only add to the troubles that an afflicted person already has at home, school, or work.

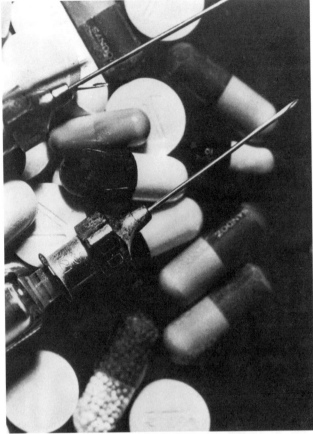

control. Panic attacks may occur.

At the same time, the individual shows a number of related symptoms. Examples include:

- Difficulty sleeping or, at the other extreme, sleeping too much. Usually, this is a problem of insomnia, or inability to sleep. The troubled individual may have difficulty falling asleep after going to bed (this is called "initial insomnia"). More often, he or she wakes up in the middle of the night ("middle insomnia") or too early in the morning ("terminal insomnia") and cannot go back to sleep. The opposite of insomnia is "hypersomnia." People who have that problem tend to sleep too long, or to fall asleep during the day.

- Loss of appetite, or a desire to eat all the time (especially sweets). Naturally, this can result in a noticeable weight loss or gain.

- The person may seem to be very nervous and squirms constantly, paces the floor, wrings hands, pulls at clothes or hair, or rubs the skin. When spoken to or asked a question, the person may seem distracted, slow to answer or to act; the response, when it comes, may be hard to hear or understand.

- Loss of concentration and energy. An excellent worker may become sloppy. It may take twice as long as it should to get dressed in the morning or to eat a meal. The person may become more forgetful (this is especially common with older people who are depressed). Everyday problems and tasks may be unusually hard to handle. For students, the result can be declining grades, cutting class, or even dropping out of school. For adults, the result can be the loss of a job or problems in a marriage.

- Feelings of uselessness or guilt. A casual remark can be taken the wrong way; although no criticism was intended, it can make the individual feel inferior or believe he or she has done something wrong. Even if a problem is caused by something no one could predict or control, this individual might feel responsible. It's common to see the depressed person assume personal blame for the problems, illness, or death of a loved one. The individual might feel personally responsible for faraway crimes, disasters, war, or world hunger. Meanwhile, actual failures or mistakes made long ago may come back to haunt the person.

A major depressive episode is an extended condition. All of us have depressing days. We even have longer periods of sadness or anxiety about various crises that are part of life. But people experiencing a major depressive episode have not just one bad day, or two, or five, but at least two straight weeks of them. The symptoms are present most of the day, almost every day.

For some individuals the episode is mild, for others severe. In mild cases, the person may be able to hide the depression and act normally, but it is a struggle to put up this front. In severe cases, the person may become unable to do simple things like dress or brush his or her teeth.

All this can lead to drug or alcohol abuse, and to very dark thoughts of death and suicide. Sometimes people in this state of mind consider suicide only for a moment, then put the thought away quickly. With others, the notion returns, perhaps several times a week. "The world would be better off without me," they reason. Or they might feel overwhelmed by problems and want to give up. In serious cases, they actually may obtain a gun, rope, or dangerous drugs or medications. They may plan a time and place to take their lives. In the worst situations, they actually make the attempt to commit suicide. Some succeed.

It's hard for counselors to know which depressives are in a "high-risk" group—that is, which ones might actually attempt suicide. Some studies indicate the likelihood of suicide cannot accurately be predicted.

It is also hard for caregivers to understand the subject's exact frame of mind if a physical ailment also exists. One patient may respond slowly to questions and commands because he has suffered a stroke, not because of depression. Another patient may have gained a lot of weight because she is diabetic. Or a person may be tired all the time because of cancer, not because of a mental or emotional problem. And with older people, it can be hard for a counselor to distinguish between depression and a condition known as dementia, or mental deterioration.

Some of the symptoms of a major depressive episode are the same as those of grief over the loss of a loved one—a normal stage in everyone's life. At the same time, other troubles in a person's life, such as grief or disease, might trigger a major depressive episode or another type of psychological disorder.

Factors that differentiate normal sadness from abnormal depression include the severity and duration of the symptoms and how deeply they affect the person's life.

Family, friends, or teachers can often tell if a person is undergoing a major depressive episode. It may be obvious in the facial expression. The individual may break down and cry when discussing how he or she feels. A person who always has loved to listen to music, or swim, or play chess may stop doing those things for no apparent reason and make up elaborate excuses to avoid doing them. A friend or relative who usually is pleasant to be around may become snappy or angry at minor annoyances.

Yet the person may deny feeling sad and say with a shrug, "I just feel blah." Or the hurting individual may complain about headaches, stomachaches, or other pains, but deny mental or emotional problems.

It is estimated that 10 to 15 percent of young people who experience

Ten to 15 percent of manic depressives attempt suicide because of their mental problems. Tragically, some succeed.

major depressive episodes will go on to develop bipolar I disorder, which is described in the next chapter.

MIXED EPISODE

A mixed episode includes symptoms of a manic episode and a major depressive episode. These symptoms, which appear more often in young people than in older adults, are obvious almost every day for at least a week.

Perhaps it's here that the term "manic depression" is understood most clearly. The person's mood shifts unexpectedly between ecstasy and sadness or testiness. We see evidence of both manic episodes and major depressive episodes close together.

Some or all of the following things may happen:

- Eating habits become very irregular.
- The person has trouble sleeping and is agitated during the waking hours.
- The person does unexplainable things and thinks about committing suicide.
- The individual becomes confused easily.

Feeling very unhappy, this person often asks for help. People suffering from manic episodes are much less likely to request help, because they don't realize things are very wrong.

A mixed episode can last for weeks or months. It is a serious situation. This kind of behavior can cause a person to lose friends or a job or to fail in school.

Like many related disturbances, the mixed episode can be mistaken for drug abuse or medical reactions. Sometimes those other problems are, in fact, going on in the person's life. Doctors recognize these combined ailments as, for example, substance-induced mood disorders with mixed features—but they are not the same as mixed episodes. Still, some experts believe that people who experience manic or depressive symptoms after being treated for certain types of medical problems are more likely than others to have true mood disorder episodes later. This is especially a concern with young patients.

Sometimes manic episodes or major depressive episodes turn into mixed episodes. For example, the person may undergo several weeks of manic symptoms followed by a period of both manic and depressive moods. Doctors are careful to note the exact sequence of behaviors. The sequence just mentioned, for example, would be termed bipolar I disorder, most recent episode mixed.

On the other hand, mixed episodes can become major depressive episodes. They also can change to manic episodes, but this is not very common.

As you can see, mixed episodes involve very complicated patterns of behavior. They also resemble the attention deficit/hyperactivity disorder mentioned earlier.

Determining the differences between a mixed episode and so many similar conditions is not easy. It takes extremely careful, thorough study to determine exactly which variation of an illness is attacking a patient. Professionals must gather and evaluate all the clinical information they can learn about each case, considering the patient's behavior history as well as interviews, physical examination, and laboratory tests.

■   ■   ■

At the beginning of this chapter, you learned there are different types of bipolar disorders. To distinguish them, you first must understand what goes on during each of the mood episodes. The next chapter will look generally at each of the bipolar disorders.

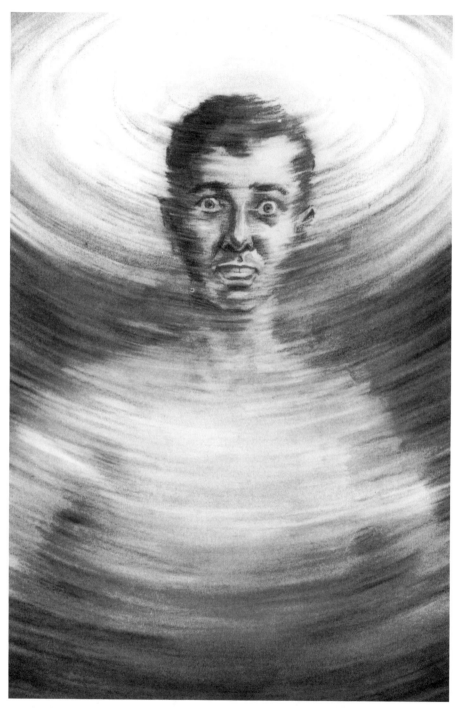

Mood episodes—manic, hypomanic, major depressive, and mixed episodes—are present in all people with manic depression. The types of episodes that occur in each patient determine the category of bipolar disorder.

4

HOW EPISODES ARE INTERRELATED

Now that we have discussed the four kinds of "mood episodes" involved in manic depression, let's see how doctors categorize bipolar disorders. The categorization depends on the combination of mood episodes. You may want to refer back to the descriptions in the last chapter as we study these different illnesses. In a nutshell, the types of bipolar disorders can be described as follows:

- Some people experience one or more manic or mixed episode, and they usually suffer major depressive episodes as well. This is known as bipolar I disorder.

- Bipolar II disorder is diagnosed when the person undergoes at least one major depressive episode and one hypomanic episode.

- A cyclothymic disorder is determined when the person shows both hypomanic symptoms and depressive symptoms many times for at least two years. However, these symptoms aren't severe enough to be considered true manic or major depressive episodes.

- Sometimes a person has an assortment of manic and depressive problems, but the symptoms don't add up to any of the above three classifications or to a similar illness. This is called a bipolar disorder not otherwise specified

Let's examine each of the bipolar disorders more closely.

BIPOLAR I DISORDER

As we said, bipolar I disorders involve at least one manic episode or mixed episode. Sometimes individuals suffering from this disease have also experienced one or more major depressive episodes.

Bipolar I disorder is known as a "recurrent disorder." That means people

A person diagnosed with bipolar I disorder may exhibit violent behavior, such as child or spousal abuse, during severe manic episodes. This woman was homeless after leaving her abusive husband.

aren't likely to have just one episode in their lifetimes. More than 90 percent of the people who experience a manic episode will have more episodes later. Before obtaining treatment, the average person with this problem experiences four episodes in a 10-year period. The older a person gets, the more frequently the episodes occur.

But a small percentage of people with bipolar I disorder undergo as many as four or more mood episodes in a year. This pattern is called "rapid cycling."

Psychiatrists have discovered some interesting things about manic depression patterns. They know that about two-thirds of manic episodes develop just before or just after a major depressive episode.

And any given patient is likely to follow the same pattern in a cycle: manic episodes for that person probably will come either before or after major depressive episodes each time. Between episodes, most patients return to normal.

The *DSM-IV* provides a plain, disturbing summary of some of the worst things that can happen to people with bipolar I disorder—and to those around them:

> Completed suicide occurs in 10%-15% of individuals with Bipolar I Disorder. Child abuse, spouse abuse, or other violent behavior may occur during severe Manic Episodes or during those with psychotic features. Other associated problems include school truancy, school failure, occupational failure, divorce, or episodic antisocial behavior.

BIPOLAR II DISORDER

Bipolar II disorder is marked by one or more major depressive episodes and one or more hypomanic episodes. If a patient has experienced a manic or mixed episode, the diagnosis cannot be bipolar II disorder. This disorder is severe enough to cause a person serious problems with work, school, and social life.

In bipolar II disorder, about two-thirds of the hypomanic episodes happen just before or after a major depressive episode. As with bipolar I disorder, a person will experience the different types of episodes in repeated patterns. And as with bipolar I, the episodes probably will occur more frequently as the person grows older. Also, as with bipolar I disorder, a small percentage of people with bipolar II disorder experience rapid cycling: four or more hypomanic or major depressive episodes a year.

Most people with bipolar II disorder return to normal after an episode. But an estimated 15 percent continue to exhibit unstable moods, with related personal problems that can affect social life, studies, and jobs.

With bipolar II disorder, psychosis (schizophrenia or other forms of mental derangement) isn't present during the hypomanic episodes. Furthermore, psychosis is less common during the major depressive episodes of bipolar II disorder than during those episodes of bipolar I disorder.

Other fine lines must be drawn in diagnosing this illness accurately.

For example, people coming out of a major depressive episode often experience "euthymia," a peculiar feeling of joy or peace of mind that can last several days. It's important that counselors not confuse euthymia with a hypomanic episode in the wake of a major depressive episode.

Bipolar II disorder is not the same as the illnesses known as major depressive disorder and dysthymic disorder. Bipolar II disorder involves a lifetime history of at least one hypomanic episode.

Various mental disorders (different from mood disorders) are associated with bipolar II disorder. They include substance abuse, anorexia nervosa and bulimia, attention deficit/hyperactivity disorder, panic disorder, social phobia, and borderline personality disorder.

Just how serious is bipolar II disorder? Again quoting from the *DSM-IV*:

> Completed suicide (usually during Major Depressive Episodes) is a significant risk, occurring in 10%-15% of persons with Bipolar II Disorder. School truancy, school failure, occupational failure, or divorce may be associated with Bipolar II Disorder.

CYCLOTHYMIC DISORDER

A person suffering from a cyclothymic disorder experiences ongoing mood changes. There are periods of both hypomanic and depressive symptoms. The symptoms aren't numerous, severe, or long enough to be called manic or major depressive episodes, but they do cause distress and they can affect the person's social life, studies, job, and other activities.

For two years or longer, an adult with this disorder enjoys freedom from these symptoms for no more than two months at a time. Children and teenagers can be diagnosed with this disorder after one year of symptoms. Cyclothymic disorder involves no major depressive, manic, or mixed episodes, but it is serious enough.

Initially, a person usually displays the symptoms of cyclothymic disorder as a teenager or young adult. In many cases it develops gradually, almost unnoticeably. When this occurs in an older person, doctors sometimes suspect a connection to what is known as mood disorder due to a general medical condition (multiple sclerosis, for example).

The pattern of mood swings may resemble other ailments like schizoaffective disorder or psychotic disorders (schizophrenia or delu-

Two students talk outside Henry Ford II Senior High School in Sterling Heights, Michigan, in October 1997. Over a period of a few weeks, five students at the school committed suicide, leaving parents and teachers confused about their motives. Suicide can be one of the effects of bipolar II disorder, along with failure in school or in a job.

sional disorder, for example). Psychiatrists must try to determine whether the symptoms truly indicate a cyclothymic disorder, or perhaps are "associated features" of a psychotic disorder. And as with other types of mood disorder, the symptoms are much the same as with certain signs of medication and drug abuse.

An individual suffering from cyclothymic disorder might be thought of by others simply as "moody." (Of course, this doesn't mean that everyone who seems moody has cyclothymic disorder. We all are moody at times.) The person might be unreliable or impossible to predict. Although the condition is not as radical as other types of mood disorder, it is serious enough to call for treatment. And there is a chance the person at some point will develop bipolar I or II disorder.

Cyclothymic disorders are sometimes easy to mistake for substance-induced mood disorders. Of course, with drugs, the mood changes usually stop after the person stops using the drugs.

THE DIFFICULTY OF DIAGNOSIS

Psychiatrists have to be very careful with their diagnoses. Every factor, even the smallest, must be considered. Professionals who understand moods know that there is no cut-and-dried diagnosis of mood disorders. Many psychological disorders outside the scope of this volume have similar characteristics, especially in young people. These include such conditions as schizoaffective disorder, schizophrenia, delusional disorder, and others. Experienced counselors never rush to judgment in determining the exact nature of the person's ailment.

Individuals sometimes go several months or longer without showing manic symptoms. Doctors try to identify the most recent type of episode the patient has experienced. After they investigate, the doctors might specify their findings as, for example, bipolar I disorder, most recent episode manic or bipolar I disorder, most recent episode depressed.

Clinicians must go further in pinpointing the nature of the patient's condition. They might describe the most recent episode (or the current condition, if the patient is undergoing an episode) as "severe with psychotic features" or "mild" or "moderate." They might record that an episode is "in partial remission" or even "in full remission." Major depressive episodes might be termed "chronic" (that is, fairly continuous for a long period of time). There may be "catatonic features" or "melancholic features." These terms are all called specifiers.

It's important that all doctors use the same system of recording what they find. The order in which they identify specifiers and collective traits of a patient's condition is not haphazard. A less-complex case might be recorded as "bipolar I disorder, single manic episode, mixed." A more involved finding might read "bipolar I disorder, most recent episode depressed, severe with psychotic features, with melancholic features, with rapid cycling."

How might a psychiatrist evaluate information about a patient he believed was manic depressive? Suppose, for example, Erin from Chapter Three has undergone only one manic episode—and the doctor is confident it was a true manic episode, not a delusional disorder or similar illness. Because Erin has no past history of major depressive episodes, the doctor would probably diagnose the case as bipolar I disorder, single manic episode. Specifics may be added to this diagnosis, depending on the details of Erin's episode.

Here's another example. Jill, a patient undergoing a hypomanic episode, has in the past experienced one or more manic or mixed episodes. These mood prob-

A patient discusses her feelings with a doctor who is helping her cope with mental illness. Psychiatrists must be careful in diagnosing manic depression. Every factor of the person's behavior and feelings must be considered, and the doctor must be cautious not to mistake one disorder for another, as many psychological disorders have similar characteristics.

lems were serious enough to affect her school performance, to injure her relationships with other people, or to embarrass her in public. If the doctor believes these problems are true hypomanic, manic, and/or mixed episodes—not psychotic disorders that carry similar symptoms—he would diagnose her as bipolar I disorder, most recent episode hypomanic.

In a third case, Dennis recently went through a major depressive episode that the doctor has decided was not a psychotic disorder with similar symptoms. In the past, Dennis has had one or more manic or mixed episodes. The doctor will probably diagnose Dennis's condition as bipolar I disorder, most recent episode depressed. The doctor might note "with melancholic features" or another specifier, depending on Dennis's case.

As you can see, there is no easy diagnosis of mood disorders, because all cases, like all people, are different.

Cyclothymic disorders may also seem to be bipolar I or bipolar II disorders with rapid cycling. But the moods in cyclothymic disorders aren't quite the same as those in major depressive, manic, or mixed episodes.

Sometimes, though, a major depressive, manic, or mixed episode occurs in a patient who has a proven cyclothymic disorder. In that case, both a cyclothymic disorder and bipolar I or bipolar II disorder will be diagnosed.

BIPOLAR DISORDER
NOT OTHERWISE SPECIFIED

Sometimes a person demonstrates manic depressive symptoms, but overall their symptoms don't fit any of the bipolar disorders described above. Doctors refer to this condition as bipolar disorder not otherwise specified.

The person may undergo several days of combined manic and depressive symptoms, but the episodes don't last as long as a manic or major depressive episode. He or she might experience a succession of hypomanic episodes, but there is no apparent depression, which could qualify the problem as bipolar II disorder. Or the individual might experience a manic or mixed episode that is "superimposed," as doctors say, on a type of psychotic disorder.

And there are times when the clinician, after weighing the information carefully, simply concludes a bipolar disorder exists but cannot say for sure whether it is the person's main problem. The patient might have an overriding medical condition, for example, or a problem with medication or drug abuse.

■   ■   ■

Each of these bipolar disorders is a form of manic depression. Many other people are terribly depressed, but it would be wrong to call their problems manic depression. Rather, the illness might be major depressive disorder, in which the person suffers major depressive episodes but not manic or hypomanic episodes. Or it may be dysthymic disorder, in which the person is depressed most of the time for years on end, but never actually experiences a major depressive episode.

Researchers study possible relationships between bipolar disorder and chemical imbalances in the brain, trying to determine if these two conditions are related or separate. Their findings could someday lead to more effective treatment (Everman and Stoudmire 1994).

Over the years, a patient's diagnosis may change. As we've seen, for example, bipolar II disorder does not involve manic or mixed episodes, whereas bipolar I disorder does. But later, if a person who has been diagnosed with bipolar II disorder suffers a manic or mixed episode (a small percentage of bipolar II individuals do), that person would now be diagnosed with bipolar I disorder.

In the same way, cyclothymic disorder may involve hypomanic and depressive symptoms that don't really add up to a major depressive episode. In this way cyclothymic disorder is similar to bipolar II disorder, but bipolar II disorder includes at least one actual major depressive episode. If a person is diagnosed with cyclothymic disorder and, perhaps several years later, suffers a major depressive episode, doctors add the diagnosis of bipolar II disorder.

Finally, there are certain kinds of mood disorders that simply cannot be categorized. The experts label them mood disorders not otherwise specified.

Most doctors and researchers believe that manic depression is genetic—passed from parent to child.

5

CAUSES AND INFLUENTIAL FACTORS

What causes manic depression?

Psychiatrists and others have been trying to answer that question for generations. The best evidence tells us the disease is transmitted genetically, from parent to child. If a person's parents or close relatives suffered from manic depression, chances are that the person will have the disorder as well.

Evidence to that effect was established in the early 20th century. More recent studies have shown both bipolar and unipolar (depression) disorders to be "highly familial" (Rieder et al. 1994).

In Chapter One, Dr. Kay Redfield Jamison, the widely renowned psychologist and author, was introduced. Dr. Jamison understands manic depression firsthand because she, too, has experienced it. Her father, a meteorologist, also experienced radical mood changes. At one point he would be elated and flighty, like a child. Later he would plunge into depression that would last for months.

Not every child of a manic depressive parent will become manic depressive. The *DSM-IV* says studies simply indicate that first-degree biological relatives have elevated rates of developing bipolar I or II disorder, compared with the general population.

Although bipolar disorders appear to be genetic, manic depressive episodes can also be triggered by certain things in daily life unrelated to genetics. The *DSM-IV* points out, for example, evidence suggesting "changes in sleep-wake schedule such as occur during time zone changes or sleep deprivation may precipitate or exacerbate" both bipolar I and bipolar II episodes.

THE STUDY OF "PSYCHIATRIC GENETICS"

Drs. Ronald O. Rieder, Charles A. Kaufmann, and James A. Knowles outlined the aims of genetic research in psychiatry in the *American Psychiatric Press Textbook of Psychiatry*. Paraphrased, these goals are:

1. To identify the "genetic component" of the causes of psychiatric disorders. It is hoped that this knowledge will reveal the extent to which a disorder is genetic, the resulting DNA rearrangement, abnormal characteristics of the gene(s) involved, and "the processes by which genetic abnormalities lead to symptoms."

2. To identify the "nongenetic component" of the causes of mental disorders. This knowledge may identify environmental factors that might cause or trigger disorders.

3. To study "diagnostic boundaries." This involves genetic associations between a disorder and the characteristics of the disorder that determine whether it can be inherited.

4. To identify how genetics affect traits and psychological symptoms.

5. To use our knowledge of genetics and environmental features to develop methods of preventing and treating psychiatric disorders.

It is not enough for investigators to know that an illness runs in a family. It must be demonstrated that the connection between family members actually is genetic: inherited from generation to generation.

To learn whether a disorder is caused by outside factors that affect a person's development or is genetic, researchers examine groups of twins and groups of adopted children. Twins have very similar genetic codes. If they are separated early in life and brought up in different environments, researchers can study differences between the twins to determine which characteristics may be inherited and which characteristics are a result of their environment or education. Similarly, adoption separates the greatest influence that parents have on their children—their genes—from the way they are brought up, or their environment.

Suppose not just one parent suffers from bipolar disorder, but both. When considering the history of the disease in the family lineage, this is called "bilineality." It's a common phenomenon. One of the questions clinicians are trying to resolve is whether bilineality affects a child in special ways.

However, doctors disagree about exactly how to define bilineality and

A doctor examines a sequence of genes on a DNA transparency chart. Medical professionals are attempting to identify the genetic component that causes mental illnesses, as well as nongenetic elements that may cause or contribute to these disorders, with hope for an eventual genetic cure for psychological disorders like manic depression.

how to analyze it. Some believe "a family in which both parental lines have any of the conditions which have been associated with affective disorder may be bilineal" (Simpson et al. 1992). Others say bilineality only occurs when both parents have been diagnosed with a mood disorder.

What about a person's race, sex, or other stereotypical factors? The *DSM-IV* says recent studies of bipolar I disorder indicate that a person's race and national origin have nothing to do with the occurrence of the disease. Sex, however, does seem to be significant in certain types of

As many as 20 percent of women are believed to suffer from unipolar disorder (depression), although the percentage of women suffering from manic depression is about the same as that of men, about 2 percent.

mood disorders, most notably depression.

Let's take a look at some of the known and suspected gender considerations involved in manic depression.

GENDER-RELATED TENDENCIES

Interestingly, one woman in five is believed to suffer from depression by itself (unipolar disorder). But only about two out of 100 women (roughly the same ratio as men) suffer from bipolar disorder (Leibenluft 1996).

The *DSM-IV* reports that bipolar I disorder is "approximately equally common in men and women." Bipolar II disorder seems to occur most frequently in (or is most frequently reported by) women. Cyclothymic disorder appears to occur with the same frequency in men and women, although women are more likely to seek treatment, according to the *DSM-IV*.

While the occurrence rate of manic depression may be about the same for women and men, a person's gender does seem to affect the order of appearance of the different types of episode (manic or depressive). And certain gender factors can direct the course of the illness. The *DSM-IV* says:

> The first episode in males is more likely to be a Manic Episode. The first episode in females is more likely to be a Major Depressive Episode. Women with Bipolar I Disorder have an increased risk of developing subsequent episodes (often psychotic) in the immediate postpartum period [after giving birth to a child]. Some women have their first episode during the postpartum period. . . . The premenstrual period may be associated with worsening of an ongoing Major Depressive, Manic, Mixed, or Hypomanic Episode.

In 1996, Dr. Ellen Leibenluft published a detailed review of the research into manic depression in women in the *American Journal of Psychiatry*. She cited four possible gender differences, based on collected research:

1. Women are more likely than men to suffer from rapid-cycling bipolar disorder. Possible reasons include a greater occurrence of hypothyroidism (lowered thyroid secretions, which result in lowered metabolism) and a heavier use of antidepressants than among men.

2. Bipolar women may be more prone to depression than men; men may be more prone to manic behavior than women.

3. Bipolar women may be more prone than men to dysphoric (exaggerated) mania episodes.

4. Women may develop manic depression during their late forties more often than men, although studies are inconclusive. Leibenluft says determining gender patterns in relation to a manic depressive's age when the disease first develops is the

hardest issue to document.

Rapid cycling, as we saw in Chapter 4, means a person undergoes at least four mood episodes (either depressed, manic, or hypomanic) in a year's time. Some individuals suffer a dozen or more episodes a year—at least one a month, on average. Approximately three of four rapid-cycling manic depressives are female.

WHY GENDER DISCREPANCIES ARE SIGNIFICANT

Leibenluft observes that clinicians would find it "both interesting and useful" to know whether manic depressive women have a predisposition toward depression while they are manic. That kind of potential complication in the disease is the subject of continuing research.

Another topic for further research is whether the reproductive cycle affects the course of a mood illness in manic depressive women. While many studies disclose that relapsing, psychotic illness seems to be related to menstrual cycles, not enough is known to draw definite conclusions, Leibenluft says. Nor do doctors know whether pregnancy or menopause affect the nature of bipolar disorder.

Evidence is fairly reliable concerning the likelihood of manic depressive episodes in a woman after she gives birth to a child. One study found a greater-than-20-percent risk for manic depressive women to be admitted for psychiatric treatment within a month after childbirth. Other studies have shown that euphoric symptoms in a manic depressive woman just after giving birth may predict depression weeks later.

"[T]here is no other time in the life of a male or female bipolar patient when the risk of an episode is higher than it is for a female bipolar patient in the postpartum period," Leibenluft comments. She identifies three possible risk factors that may affect rapid cycling: hypothyroidism, gonadal (sex gland) steroids, and antidepressant prescription drugs.

The question is how such factors might influence the course of episodes in a manic depressive person. For example, changes in sleep and energy levels are symptoms of manic depression. Therefore, it is of interest to study the possible effects of gonadal steroids on a person's sleep cycle.

Leibenluft points out certain evidence indicating that women generally sleep more than men. Thus, "to the extent that sleep is depres-

One of the myths that past societies believed about manic depression and other psychological disorders was that people who were poor or lived "degenerate" lives passed
negative characteristics, such as mental illness, to their children. William Hogarth's 1754
illustration Gin Lane depicts popular stereotypes about the lives of the lower classes
in London.

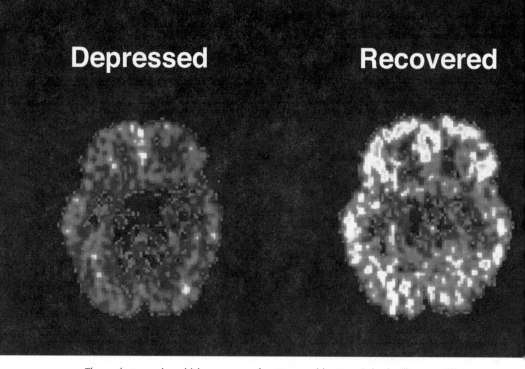

Depressed **Recovered**

These photographs, which are scans of a 45-year-old woman's brain, illustrate differences in the brain that occur during depressed periods. These positron-emission tomography (PET) scans show that depression is associated with brain dysfunction in several areas, particularly the frontal and temporal lobes. The scan on the left was taken when the patient was on no medication and was very depressed. The one on the right was taken several months later, after her depression had been treated with medication. The lighter areas show that the entire brain is more active after successful treatment.

sogenic . . . this gender difference may contribute to women's greater risk of depression."

The belief that antidepressant medication can cause rapid cycling in manic depressives is debated. If it is true, then the fact that more women than men are treated for depression might help account for the greater tendency of female manic depressives toward rapid cycling.

Leibenluft concludes, "Obviously, the development of an antidepressant that does not precipitate either mania or rapid cycling would be a major advance in the treatment of bipolar illness."

MYTHS ABOUT MANIC DEPRESSION

Through generations, doctors and others have speculated about why certain people suffer from mania and depression and others don't. Their conclusions have played a major role in how the patients of their times have been treated.

Dr. Norman Dain reports that some psychiatrists in the 19th century embraced the idea of "degeneration" as the cause of insanity.

> According to this theory, people who lived degenerate lives transmitted to their offspring, by heredity, environmentally acquired negative characteristics, which would thus ensure chronicity and even ultimate extinction of the family line. The insane, especially those of lower-class origins, were depicted as the rejects of Darwinian evolution, congenitally unresponsive to therapy. (Dain 1994)

Imagine the kind of treatment—or nontreatment—these unfortunate individuals must have received.

Into the 20th century, some psychiatrists looked down on mental patients and the asylums and hospitals where they were kept. Dr. Adolf Meyer, a famous neuropsychiatrist who criticized this attitude, wrote, "Who wonders, then, that we still hear most people talk of the 'stigma,' as soon as mental disease or hospital is mentioned, if many physicians themselves consider the hospital merely a place of last resort?"

Then came the "mental hygiene movement" of the early 20th century. It arose as an attempt to explain the causes of mental disorders. This line of thinking gives us a good example of how theories based on inadequate research can go astray—with unhappy practical results. Dr. James W. Thompson defines it:

> The movement was based on the view that mental disorders were caused by a poor environment in childhood and by inherited deficiencies. Intervention in childhood behavior problems, largely through the schools, was believed to be required to prevent mental disorders. (Thompson 1994)

Although by modern standards this view was simplistic in its approach, it did have certain positive results. It led to the expansion of services for mental health patients: more applied social work and the development of outpatient facilities, for example. A National Committee on Mental Hygiene was established to educate the public in this area and to generate interest in children's growth and development.

Child guidance programs also were established.

But the frequency of mental health problems changed little despite these policies. As Thompson observes, "another well-meaning effort to serve mentally ill persons gradually deteriorated into pessimism."

Meanwhile, mental hygienists were following some alarming practices. Thompson writes:

> [Mental hygiene's] theories of the environmental and hereditary causation of mental disorder led many adherents to support marriage regulation, immigration restriction, and involuntary sterilization. These views had their most extreme expression in the eugenics and nativism movements of the late 19th and early 20th centuries. A total of 18,552 mentally ill persons were sterilized before opposition forces and reaction to news about atrocities in Nazi Germany brought these practices to a halt.

MODERN RESEARCH

Now that scientists are confident manic depression is an inherited disease, research is mounting to identify the specific gene that causes it. In 1993, a multimillion-dollar grant was given to several major research centers for this pursuit, *Hospital and Community Psychiatry* reported. The project involved collecting and comparing DNA samples from families affected by manic depression.

The quest to solve the riddle of manic depression has progressed from thinly grounded social theories to the complexities of chemical research. Sometimes it seems investigators go to a lot of trouble to determine small details. Yet it is only by following every possible path of investigation, by scrutinizing each detail of evidence, that we can understand the exact nature and causes of manic depression.

Over the years, among other avenues, researchers have studied the possible linkage of bipolar disorder to color blindness. This and other findings that seemed promising at first turned out to be wrong or could not be proved.

Some biological conditions seem likely candidates in explaining certain types of manic depressive behavior, but not other types. Researchers repeatedly have observed, for example, an association between low serotonin levels and violent, impulsive behavior. However, this condition does not seem to affect depression.

But researchers remain hopeful about the eventual positive results of molecular genetic strategies in this disorder.

Rieder, Kaufmann, and Knowles are optimistic about the progress of genetic research: "New techniques hold the promise of determining the location, nature, and product of the genetic contribution to many disorders," they wrote in the *American Psychiatric Press Textbook of Psychiatry* in 1994.

The problems of bipolar disorder can begin at a young age. Although parents may believe their child is in a "stage" and will "grow out of" his or her behavior, a young person with manic depression will probably develop more serious problems as he or she grows older.

6

MANIC DEPRESSION IN YOUNG PEOPLE

In most people with this disease, serious episodes of bipolar disorder begin during young adulthood, but the problems can start much earlier. A young person is likely to display somewhat different symptoms of manic depression than an adult. Evaluating the symptoms in small children and teenagers can be especially confusing and difficult for clinicians.

According to the *DSM-IV*, "The core symptoms of a major depressive episode are the same for children and adolescents, although there are data that suggest that the prominence of characteristic symptoms may change with age. Certain symptoms such as somatic (bodily) complaints, irritability, and social withdrawal are particularly common in children, whereas psychomotor retardation (delays in mind/body coordination), hypersomnia (sleep irregularity), and delusions are less common in prepuberty (preteen years) than in adolescence and adulthood."

Symptoms among younger children might be irritability, emotional instability, hyperactivity, loss of sleep, and impulsive behavior. These children can't concentrate for very long and might suddenly become angry, then sulky (Weller et al. 1995).

Manic episodes among youths end more quickly than episodes of depression. A study of manic children ages 6–12 found that half showed primary signs of elation, and half showed primary signs of irritability. Nine of ten children were getting less sleep at night. Seven of ten had hallucinations and felt persecuted.

Another study indicated that young people who experience bouts of "pure depression" are slower to recover than those who experience "pure mania or mixed states" (Strober et al. 1995).

Major depressive episodes in children and teenagers usually occur along with other mental problems such as disruptive behavior and anxiety attacks. One study concluded that trying to diagnose manic depression accurately in

It is difficult to diagnose bipolar disorder in children, because the mood changes of manic depression can be interpreted as common behavior. Also, clinicians must determine when a child is simply shy, restless, or angry, and when these are symptoms of a more serious problem.

teenagers presents a serious challenge to clinicians. "Adolescent patients with Bipolar Disorder are frequently misdiagnosed as having schizophrenia or other types of psychoses" (Ghadirian and Roux 1995).

A PANDORA'S BOX OF SIMILAR DISORDERS

Manic depression is difficult to diagnose in children because normal children's behavior "resembles closely hypomanic activity and any slight variations are not apt to be noticed" (Weller et al. 1995).

In 1994 a trio of doctors published a study titled "The Confusion Between Bipolar Disorder and Schizophrenia in Youth." They studied both types of patients and found a tendency among clinicians to under-diagnose manic depression.

"The more complicated nature of early-onset bipolar disorder may be a contributing factor," they reported. Citing earlier studies, they stated, "Schizophrenia in youth has been frequently diagnosed at the expense of manic depression."

Furthermore, actual manic depression in young people may begin after a similar type of problem already has been diagnosed, the report said.

The doctors concluded, "Although operational criteria have become more precise, and there are more diagnostic categories by which to catalog a psychotic adolescent, the community continues to have more difficulties codifying severe mental illness in youth" (Carlson, et al. 1994).

To give an example of the confusion doctors encounter when diagnosing young patients, consider these issues:

- The various mood changes of manic depression might be interpreted as common childhood behavior. Mood changes among children are not at all uncommon.
- Many children are not very sociable. Some are simply shy. And all of us have to adjust as we enter adolescence and we begin fending for ourselves in the "real world."
- Some of the symptoms of substance abuse are the same as some of the symptoms of manic depression.
- The clinician must distinguish between a lack of energy caused by a mood disorder and "plain laziness." Assuming the child is not lazy, the problem may be physical, not mood-related.
- In the autumn, many students normally are apprehensive about the beginning of the school term and may behave differently than usual.
- Children often become restless or angry, some of them frequently. Clinicians must determine at what point this behavior suggests a serious disorder, and whether it is evidence of a bipolar disorder or another type of conduct disturbance.

For obvious reasons, some clinicians regard the diagnosis of mood disorders among young people to be less stable or consistent than diagnoses among adults. It is especially easy for counselors to confuse manic depression with the following disorders among young people:

- Schizophrenia, which includes psychotic symptoms, but not the hurried speech or unrealistic ideas of a manic episode.
- Attention deficit/hyperactivity disorder. Like manic depression, this can involve hyperactivity and difficulty falling asleep at night. But unlike manic symptoms, these behavioral patterns are normal for that particular child, not episodes that come and go.

- Conduct disorder. The child with conduct disorder is aggressive and may become violent. This behavior is purposeful and intended to cause harm, unlike a manic episode in which the child is usually just being mischievous and will feel guilty after the episode ends. Conduct disorder does not include psychotic behavior, hurried speech, or elaborate, impossible schemes.

Traditionally, manic depression has been regarded as an illness of adults. Comparatively limited studies have been conducted into childhood bipolar disorder. One research team commented on the reason:

> This, at least in part, stems from the general neglect of Mood Disorders in children that occurred for many years in this country. For example, childhood depression was not officially recognized in the United States until the 1975 National Institute of Mental Health (NIMH) Conference on Depression in Childhood. . . . At that conference, it was concluded that adult criteria could be used to diagnose depression in children as long as appropriate modifications to accommodate for age and stage of development were made. (Weller et al. 1995)

Those studies that have been conducted among young people have yielded somewhat contradictory results. For example, different studies have indicated different conclusions regarding the frequency of manic depression among children and teenagers.

MORE COMPLICATIONS

In some cases, parents of manic depressive children also have psychological problems. This complicates the work of the clinician trying to diagnose the child. As one source explains, "it is critical to ensure that the parents are reporting their child's symptoms and not their own symptoms" (Weller et al. 1995). Investigators need to talk to others who know the child, especially schoolteachers.

Some clinicians believe most children are unable to explain their emotions accurately. "I just don't feel good," the hurting children are likely to generalize, making it more difficult for their doctors to diagnose and treat them correctly.

However, children who display symptoms similar to manic depression but who are not really ill are likely to "grow out of it." On the other hand, data from several studies support the observation that manic chil-

A young person with bipolar disorder will probably display slightly different symptoms than an adult with the same disorder. Irritability, hyperactivity, and social withdrawal are more common among children, while sleep disorders, delusions, and problems with coordination occur more often in bipolar young adults.

dren do not "grow out" of this phase.

Meanwhile, professionals must try to identify and help those children who truly suffer from manic depression. Their work must be thorough and their observations keen. "There is no substitute for a well-trained clinician who does a comprehensive assessment," one source emphasizes. "This includes interviewing the child with the family, the child alone, and the family alone; obtaining teacher observations; and then integrating all the information to arrive at a clinical diagnosis" (Weller et al. 1995).

Clinical workers are especially eager to find and treat "high-risk" youths. These are children who suffer from depression before they reach their teens and children with family histories of mood disorders.

It's especially important in child cases to develop a broad treatment plan. As suggested above, the treatment plan might involve parents and teachers. The parents themselves may be undergoing treatment for the disorder, because as researchers have learned, affective illnesses can be inherited, as discussed in Chapter Five.

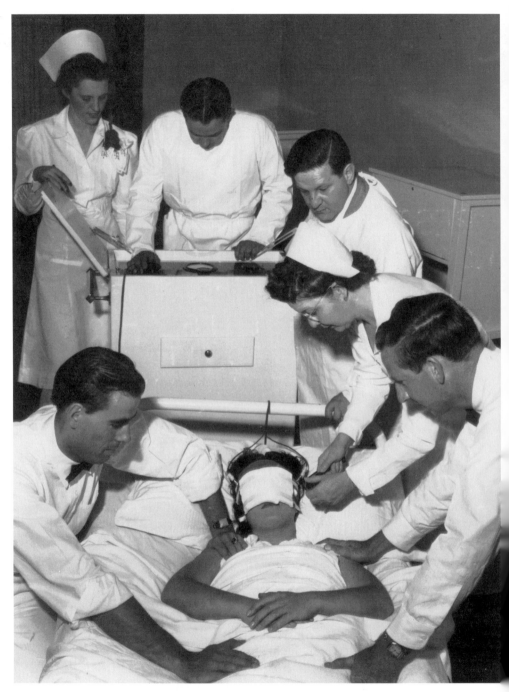

With treatment, a person with bipolar disorder can overcome the disease. The methods of treatment have changed over the years, and usually vary from patient to patient. In this 1942 photo, doctors in a California hospital are preparing to administer an electric shock treatment to a patient suffering from manic depression.

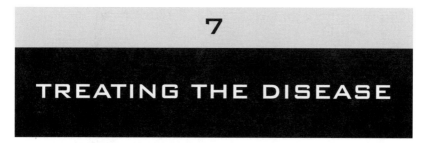

7

TREATING THE DISEASE

The good news about manic depression is that in most cases it can be treated successfully. With proper treatment, many patients enjoy "complete remission of symptoms" and return to normal, according to the *DSM-IV*. That doesn't mean they're permanently cured, however; the problem may return if the treatment stops. In other cases, treatment may only reduce the length or severity of the symptoms.

The bad news is that many people who suffer from manic depression don't try to find help. Either they don't realize they have a serious illness, they're ashamed to admit it, or they can't afford treatment.

Even when someone does request help, sometimes his or her symptoms are diagnosed incorrectly. In other cases, their care is not managed well. Patients might stop taking their medicine because it is too expensive for them, they don't like the side effects, or they don't see early results and give up. Unless the full course of medication is taken, the symptoms of the illness are likely to continue (or, if they've stopped temporarily, to return).

The results of an interesting, and in some ways troubling, study were presented at the 1993 annual meeting of the American Psychiatric Association. The study gathered information about hundreds of people suffering from manic depression. Here are some of its findings:

- Fifty-nine percent of the patients studied first experienced manic or depressive symptoms as teenagers or young children.
- More than half didn't get help for at least five years; more than one-third didn't seek help for more than 10 years.
- Seventy-three percent said they were first diagnosed as having an ailment different from manic depression.
- After the average patient finally sought treatment, eight more years passed and at least three doctors were consulted before he or she

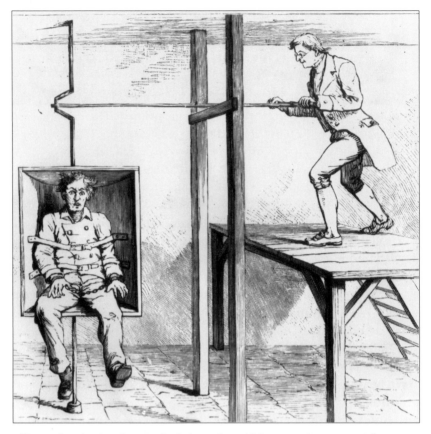

This 1818 line drawing shows a circulating swing, which was used—unsuccessfully—to treat the insane. It was believed by doctors at the time that the swing would help the depressed. "No well-regulated institution should be without one" read the original caption on the art. Today patients receive medicine and treatment that have been proven effective by decades of study.

was diagnosed correctly.

- Although medication was said to be effective in 90 percent of the patients who used it, 45 percent of those using medication had experienced recurring symptoms of the disease within the previous six months.

- A third of the patients said they didn't have the money or health insurance for proper treatment.

- Only 13 percent of manic depressives reportedly abused alcohol or drugs when their condition was under control, but 41 percent were substance abusers when their treatment was mismanaged and the disease was out of hand.

- About half believed the illness had caused permanent damage to their family relationships.

According to the National Institute of Mental Health, successful treatment is possible for more than 80 percent of people who experience major depression. But only a third try to obtain treatment, and of those who do, many are misdiagnosed and given the wrong treatment.

Treatment of manic depression is much better and more effective today than in the past. That is because the causes, influences, and general nature of the illness are understood better. Older patients may still remember times when doctors wrapped them in sheets and gave them doses of insulin to cause convulsions deliberately (Fidler 1995).

Today patients are given medication and other treatment that has been proven to work by well-documented studies. One of the first successful treatments of manic depression was in the late 19th century, when lithium was introduced. In the 1950s, chlorpromazine was found to be effective in treating both depressive and psychotic patients. Antidepressant drugs also were introduced in the 1950s, renewing medical interest in the biology of depression.

PHARMACOLOGICAL TREATMENT AND LITHIUM

Lithiucarbonate, an alkali metal often prescribed for manic depressive symptoms, was discovered in 1817 to be useful in treating a wide range of ailments. In the 1860s it began to be used for gout (inflamed joints). By the late 1880s, lithium was being prescribed for repeated depressive symptoms.

This substance produces complex effects in the brain. It also is used to treat psychiatric disorders such as schizophrenia and aggression. According to one source, "Lithium is the most widely used treatment for bipolar disorder. Although it is far from the perfect drug, it has clearly revolutionized treatment of this disorder." Sources indicate some three-fourths of manic patients treated solely with lithium respond to the treatment (Lenox and Manji 1997).

Lithium is sometimes the only prescription drug given to a person suffering from bipolar disorder. Improvement with lithium occurs gradually, during a period of days and weeks. Because of this delayed result, other medicine is often used along with lithium, especially early in the treatment, for faster relief of such symptoms as hyperactivity and insomnia. Lithium might be used in combination with carbamazepine, or with tranquilizers such as benzodiazepine, or with neuroleptic medications that are used to treat psychosis.

For the long term, lithium's effectiveness in treating bipolar disorders is well established. It diminishes both the frequency and severity of episodes. There is some evidence that lithium, if administered properly, might prevent future episodes among teenagers or at least reduce the number of relapses. Manic depressive episodes seem to occur less frequently in patients who use lithium, divalproex sodium, or carbamazepine than in those who use antidepressants or anxiolytics for treatment, according to a 1994 report in *Hospital and Community Psychiatry.*

Lithium seems to work better for some patients than for others. And patients who suffer from manic depression normally cannot just take their medicine for a while and then stop. Numerous studies have shown that half the patients who suddenly stop taking medication find themselves battling the disease again within five months (Lenox and Manji 1997).

Few medications can be taken without adverse effects. It doesn't matter what the illness and the medicine happen to be. This is no different in treating manic depression. Possible negative side effects of lithium include fatigue, nausea, weight gain, trembling, loss of memory, hair loss, and thyroid problems. Physicians must be particularly watchful for side effects when prescribing lithium in combination with another drug.

It's been shown that pharmacological treatment for manic depression may affect pregnancy. The mood stabilizers lithium, carbamazepine, and valproic acid (or valproate) may damage the development of the embryo in a small percentage of cases (Leibenluft 1996).

Carbamazepine is also known to interact with birth control medication. To be effective, greater doses of the contraceptive are required.

Doctors must also watch for the potential long-term effects of mood stabilizers on a woman's reproductive system. One study has shown that women treated for epilepsy with valproate have an unusually high incidence of certain menstrual and related problems. Lithium has been shown to have complex effects on the thyroid gland; women seem to be

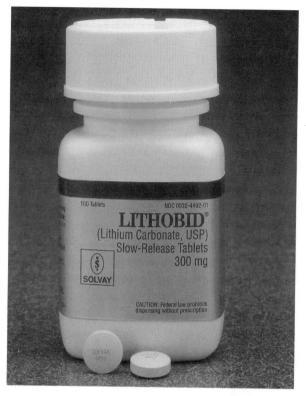

Lithium is one of the oldest treatments for manic depression, and it remains one of the most effective medications for the disease.

more susceptible to these effects than men.

Interestingly, children and teenagers seem to have fewer and less serious reactions to lithium treatment than adults.

ELECTROCONVULSIVE THERAPY

A very different kind of treatment for manic depression is electroconvulsive therapy (ECT), briefly passing an electrical shock through the patient's forehead. It has been used successfully for more than 50 years.

Electroconvulsive therapy was developed for the wrong reason, but it turned out to be effective in many cases. In the 1930s, a Hungarian psychiatrist named Meduna believed schizophrenia and epilepsy could not exist in the same person, and he tried to prove this by using chemicals, and later electrical shocks, to induce epileptic-like seizures in schizophrenic patients.

Meduna's hypothesis was later disproved, but electroconvulsive

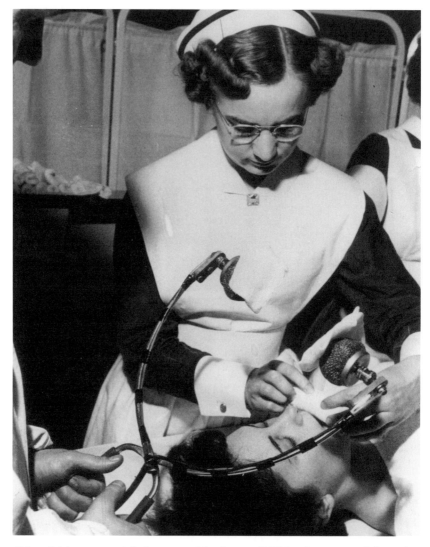

Although it is controversial, electroconvulsive therapy (ECT) has been successfully used to treat bipolar disorder for over 50 years. It is not a permanent cure, but as many as 80 percent of manic depressive patients show improvement after ECT.

therapy began to be used widely and effectively to treat both psychiatric and major mood illnesses (Weiner 1995). Induced insulin shock was also used as a form of treatment.

Doctors sometimes recommend ECT after lithium and other drugs have failed to help a patient or when the patient needs a quick response.

Often, ECT treatments are performed during a period in which the patient continues to take medication (Dantzler and Salzmon 1995).

If it succeeds, a course of electroconvulsive therapy can help send a manic or depressive episode into remission. It is not a permanent cure. But one source suggests 80 percent of manic patients show "marked improvements" after ECT (Keck et al. 1996; Weiner 1995). Electroconvulsive therapy has been used effectively to help both young and old patients.

As you can imagine, electroconvulsive therapy is not a fun thing to look forward to, although it is not particularly dangerous. Anesthesia is administered first so that the patient doesn't feel the shock. But ECT still has a negative image for some people because of the way it has been depicted in movies and on television. And it has certain side effects, including memory loss.

Although most patients have no more fear of an ECT treatment than a trip to the dentist, some patients eventually choose to take their chances with the illness rather than continue the procedure. Some think of it as "shock treatment" and associate it, in a way, with the electric chair used to execute prisoners. "I would prefer to die," said one elderly woman, refusing to undergo more ECT sessions (Fox 1994). Not even the modern-day use of muscle relaxants and anesthesia calms the anxiety of some patients about ECT.

Medication, with or without ECT treatments, usually is only part of the patient's care plan. Most individuals are given one-on-one psychotherapy and are urged to join support groups.

Dr. Kay Redfield Jamison, the professor and author whose story is told in Chapter One, believes it was psychotherapy that actually saved her from taking her own life. "Lithium moderates the illness, but therapy teaches you to live with it," she stated.

"I'm sick of her ruining our lives."

When confronted with a mental illness, many families experience a wide range of confusing and upsetting emotions. From outrage to despair, shame and denial.

They often blame victims for causing worry, embarrassment, family strife. And they can often blame themselves. "Was it my fault?" "Where did I go wrong?"

But, mental illness is no one's fault. Least of all those afflicted. It's a serious medical illness that affects one in four families—afflicting 35 million Americans from all walks of life.

Recognizing the warning signs and seeking

professional treatment for your loved one can be the first steps to reducing family fears and confusion. And to actually healing the sickness.

Today, mental illness need not be hopeless. Due to recent progress in research and treatment, two out of three victims can get better and lead productive lives.

But they can't do it alone. They need your compassion, support, and understanding.

Learn more. For an informative booklet, write: The American Mental Health Fund, P.O. Box 17700, Washington, D.C. 20041. Or call toll free: 1-800-433-5959.

 Learn to see the sickness. Learning is the key to healing.

THE AMERICAN MENTAL HEALTH FUND

CM-5-87

UNDERSTANDING MENTAL ILLNESS CAMPAIGN
MAGAZINE AD NO. UMI-2142-86—7" x 10" (110 Screen)
Volunteer Agency: Warwick Advertising, Inc., Volunteer Coordinator: Kim Armstrong, AT&T Communications

There is a stigma attached to mood disorders such as manic depression. However, as this ad that was part of a 1987 campaign by the American Mental Health Fund points out, people suffering from bipolar disorder or other mental illness need support from family and friends in addition to medicine and therapy.

8

"WHERE DO WE FIT IN SOCIETY ?"

The plight of an alcoholic is very sad. Not only can the physical effects of long-term alcohol abuse itself shorten the person's life, but the embarrassing things alcoholism causes the person to do are humiliating. These actions may seem comical to witnesses, but to the person who does them, they are not funny at all afterward.

The situation is the same for the drug addict, who trades a short period of euphoria for a long period of damaging side effects. Perhaps the worst moment is when the person realizes the situation is out of control. From that time on, it's not that the drug addict won't stop, but rather that he or she can't stop and finally knows it.

A stigma is attached to alcoholism and drug abuse. In addition to the physical danger, there is shame. Substance abusers don't want society to know they have a problem beyond their control.

Similarly, people with mood disorders don't want to admit they have a problem they can't control. The very idea of requiring treatment for an illness like manic depression carries a stigma. It's the notion of "mental frailty." No one wants to be known as a mental case.

In the early days of hospitals and asylums, and well into the 20th century, the specter of violent patients restrained by straitjackets is how many people thought of mental illness. During the last few decades, depiction of electroconvulsive therapy has been somewhat alarming. Worried by dramatizations they've seen in movies or on television, some patients fear ECT might cause brain damage or death. If they do undergo the treatment, they usually don't care to announce it to the world. For example, in 1972, Thomas Eagleton, a popular senator from Minnesota, was selected as George McGovern's running mate in the presidential election. However, after the media reported Eagleton had undergone electroconvulsive therapy for depression several years earlier, the senator had to withdraw from the race because of the negative connections

MENTAL ILLNESS AND THE MOVIES

Hollywood has portrayed mental illness in many ways over the years. In the 1967 film *Valley of the Dolls*, Patty Duke played Neely O'Hara, an actress with mental problems whose career was destroyed by alcohol and drugs. Duke herself suffers from bipolar disorder. The 1975 film *One Flew Over the Cuckoo's Nest*, which starred Jack Nicholson, depicted life in an insane asylum. The film won Oscar Awards for Best Picture, Best Actor, Best Actress, Best Director, and Best Screenplay. In 1994, Jessica Lange played a woman who suffers from bipolar disorder in the movie *Blue Sky*; she won an Oscar for her performance. Some early Hollywood films that are notable for dealing with mental illness include *The Snake Pit* (1948), which starred Olivia de Havilland as a patient in a mental institution and was one of the first films to deal with mental breakdowns and the process of recovery, and *The Three Faces of Eve* (1957), about a woman with multiple personalities.

Valley of the Dolls

One Flew Over the Cuckoo's Nest

Blue Sky

people made between Eagleton and a mental illness.

Manic depression can have a horrible impact on the lives of people who suffer from the disease—and the lives of those around them. If a person admits the problem and seeks help, treatment can be very expensive. Yet without treatment, the toll can be far greater. The costs become physical, emotional, social, and financial. For example, the uncontrolled spending sprees described as part of manic episodes can wreck family budgets.

There's more to consider. If adults are abusive to their spouses or children, they literally can lose their families. They not only may lose custody of their children, but may be legally forbidden to visit them.

Naturally, manic depressives have terrible self-doubts. "I have the self-esteem of an earthworm," one individual told a support group (Fidler 1995).

The way these people are viewed by society does little to improve their self-images. While racist and sexist jokes are frowned upon today, jokes about the mentally ill continue to be told and approved in many circles. Popular horror movies often stereotype mentally disturbed characters.

WHAT IS A STIGMA?

A stigma, by one definition, is a "mark of shame."

People for centuries regarded most mentally ill people as violent, unmanageable, and incurable. Many clergymen thought ministers, rather than doctors, should deal with disturbed individuals, because mental problems commonly were thought to be spiritual in nature. The cause, they believed, was demonic possession. Exorcism, an attempt to purge evil spirits with rituals, was the logical response. A stigma remains attached to mood disorders, and society still looks down upon those it affects.

Dr. Norman Dain, writing in *Hospital & Community Psychiatry* in 1994, defines stigma as:

> [T]he attribution of prejudicial characteristics to a whole class of people, "branding" all of them. . . . Stigmatization of the "insane" has an ancient history, which began at least as early as biblical times, when the tradition of madness as demonic possession and punishment for sin became codified in religious belief and practice.

In modern generations, Dain says, the stigma of mental illness has been complicated by a movement known as "antipsychiatry." Who are antipsychiatrists, and what are they about? Dain describes:

> At various times these groups have included neurologists, social workers, new religions, consumers, and psychiatrists themselves. Their common ground has been objection to psychiatry as a hospital-centered medical specialty legally authorized to institutionalize and treat patients.

HOW—AND WHERE—SHOULD THE MENTALLY ILL BE TREATED?

Let's consider briefly several developments during the evolution of "institutional" care for the mentally ill.

First, during the late 1800s, heredity began to be strongly suspected as a factor in mental illness.

Second, some professionals believed a person's living conditions could cause or aggravate these disorders. In either case, psychiatrists started to doubt whether the person's life could be restored to normal. Hospitals and asylums became "custodial" in nature, simply housing the patients, many of whom were in chains or straitjackets much of the time.

Third, the medical specialty of neurology, the study of the human nervous system, evolved during and just after the Civil War. Some neurologists believed they could treat patients who had mental problems more effectively outside the institutions than could psychiatrists inside asylums. A few neurologists said asylums were "unnecessary and destructive to patients" (Quen 1994).

Today, 80 percent of the people diagnosed with manic depression can be successfully treated, allowing them to live normal lives outside of hospitals or asylums. Only the most severe cases are unable to fit into society and require institutionalization.

COUNTING THE COSTS

While issues of treatment and care for persons with psychological disorders such as manic depression have been debated for many years, an indisputable fact is that mental disorders are very expensive. The National Institute of Mental Health has estimated that treatment of mental disorders alone costs more than $67 billion a year in the United States. That figure is more than doubled if we consider the millions of hours of lost work, payments for disability claims, and social service costs.

A 1993 report from the National Mental Health Association (NMHA), based on 1990 statistics, found that depression caused more worker absenteeism—some 29 million lost work weeks in 1990—than any other illness except advanced arterial diseases. A related study indicated that the cost to employers that year was $3,000 in absentee costs for each depressed worker.

The NMHA study found that 11 million Americans suffered from some form of depression in 1990. Seventy-one percent were women; more than half were age 30 to 44.

Of the 11 million people suffering from depression, 1.8 million were manic depressive.

OLD PROBLEMS CONTINUE

In some ways, the problems faced by care providers 100 years ago remain the same today. For example, what becomes of the poor when they are discharged from mental health institutions? Some are numbered among today's homeless.

One commentator, Dr. James W. Thompson, cautions against a coming "dark age" in public support for mental health services. He believes "negative attitudes about mental illness continue to drive public policy." Policy makers, Thompson says, are influenced by "ancient themes of misconception and fear about mental disorder, cloaked in the more socially acceptable garb of 'cost-efficiency' and 'managed care.'"

In the "frenzy to control health care costs," some services have already been discontinued, Thompson points out. "As long as policy makers continue to believe that mental disorder is moral weakness and that treatment of mental disorder is ineffective and too costly, swings from enlightenment to darkness will continue, and mentally ill patients will remain at the mercy of political expediency" (Thompson 1994).

But overall, their plight is better today because of better understanding and better medication. One study concludes, "Complete 'cures' are perhaps as infrequent as ever, but most researchers would agree that the number of patients who are able to return to the community has greatly increased, that human rights are more closely watched, and that hospital stays have been considerably shortened" (Evenson et al. 1994).

Modern treatment has shown that patients indeed can be helped. Hopefully, in time this success will diminish the stigma attached to mental disorders.

Social support is vital to those suffering from manic depression. They must cope with an illness that is very serious and can be dangerous. It may take them years to admit they have a problem. When they do seek help, they may face misunderstanding and even ridicule by those who know them. Some people have the idea that mental illness is not treatable or not worth treating.

Overcoming the stigma is much the same with all forms of psychological or mental ailments. It takes a lot of courage for a person to acknowledge the illness and get the necessary treatment.

APPENDIX

FOR MORE INFORMATION

American Academy of Child & Adolescent Psychiatry
3615 Wisconsin Ave. NW
Washington, DC 20016
(202) 966-7300
Web site: www.aacap.org/web/aacap

American Academy of Psychiatry & the Law
P.O. Box 30
Bloomfield, CT 06002
(800) 331-1389, (203) 242-5450,
fax (203) 286-0787
Web site: www.cc.emory.edu/AAPL

American Medical Association
515 North State Street
Chicago, IL 60610
(312) 464-5000
Web site: www.ama-assn.org

American Psychiatric Association
1400 K Street NW
Washington, DC 20005
(202) 682-6062
Web site: www.psych.org

Canadian Mental Health Association
970 Lawrence Avenue West, Suite 205
Toronto, Ontario
Canada M6A 3B6
(416)789-7957, fax (416)789-9079
Web site: www3.sympatico.ca/cmha.toronto

The Dana Foundation
745 Fifth Avenue, Suite 700
New York, NY 10151
(212) 223-4040
Web site: www.dana.org

Depression and Related Affective Disorders Association
Meyer 3-181
600 N. Wolfe Street
Baltimore MD 21287-7381
(410) 955-4647, fax (410) 614-3241
Web site: infonet.welch.jhu.edu/
departments/drada/default

National Alliance for the Mentally Ill
200 N. Glebe Road
Suite 1015
Arlington, VA 22203-3754
(800) 950-6264, (703) 524-7600,
fax (703) 524-9094
Web site: www.nami.org

National Depressive and Manic Depressive Association
730 Franklin Street, Suite 501
Chicago, IL 60610
(800) 826-3632, (312) 642-0049,
fax (312) 642-7243
Web site: www.ndmda.org

National Foundation for Depressive Illness
P.O. Box 2257
New York, NY 10116
(800) 248-4344, (212) 268-4260,
fax (212) 268-4434
Web site: www.social.com/health/nhic/
data/hr2300/hr2374.html

National Institute of Mental Health
Public Inquiries, Room 7C-02
5600 Fishers Lane
Rockville, MD 20857
(301) 496-4000
Web site: www.nimh.nih.gov

National Mental Health Association
1021 Prince Street
Alexandria, VA 22314-2971
(800) 969-6642, (703) 684-7722,
fax (703) 684-5968
Web site: www.aoa.dhhs.gov/aoa/
dir/181.html

**Stanley Center for the Innovative Treatment
of Bipolar Disorder**
3811 O'Hara Street
Pittsburgh, PA 15213
(800) 424-7657, (412) 624-2476
Web site: www.wpic.pitt.edu/research/
stanley/stanley.htm

APPENDIX

SOURCES CITED

Alessi, Norman, Michael W. Naylor, Mohammad Ghaziuddin, and Jon Kar Zubieta. "Update on Lithium Carbonate Therapy in Children and Adolescents," *Journal of the American Academy of Child and Adolescent Psychiatry* 33, no. 3 (March 1994).

Alger, Ian. "Two Documentaries." *Hospital and Community Psychiatry* 45, no. 6 (June 1994).

Amaranth, Emily. "On Alleged 'Remission' from Severe Bipolar Disorder." *Hospital and Community Psychiatry* 45, no. 10 (October 1994).

American Psychiatric Association. "Mood Disorders." *Diagnostic and Statistical Manual of Mental Disorders*, 4th edition. Washington, D.C.: American Psychiatric Press, 1994.

———. "Mood Disorders." *Treatment of Psychiatric Disorders*, 2nd edition. 2 vols. Washington, D.C.: American Psychiatric Press, 1995.

Carlson, Gabrielle A., Shmuel Fennig, and Evelyn J. Bromet. "The Confusion between Bipolar Disorder and Schizophrenia in Youth: Where Does It Stand in the 1990s?" *Journal of the American Academy of Child and Adolescent Psychiatry* 33, no. 5 (May 1994).

Coughlin, George Gordon. *Your Introduction to Law*, 4th edition. New York: Barnes & Noble Books, 1983.

Dain, Norman. "Reflections on Antipsychiatry and Stigma in the History of American Psychiatry." *Hospital and Community Psychiatry* 45, no. 10 (October 1994).

Dantzler, Anne, and Carl Salzman. "Treatment of Bipolar Depression." *Psychopharmacology* 46, no. 3 (1995).

De bruyn, An, Karin Mendelbaum, Lodewijk A. Sandkuijl, Veronique Delvenne, Denis Hirsch, Luc Staner, Julien Mendlewicz, and Christine Van Broeckhoven. "Nonlinkage of Bipolar Illness to Tyrosine Hydroxylase, Tyrosinase, and D2 and D4 Dopamine Receptor Genes on Chromosome

11." *American Journal of Psychiatry* 151, no. 1 (January 1994).

Evenson, Richard C., Richard A. Holland, and Dong W. Cho. "A Psychiatric Hospital 100 Years Ago, Part I: A Comparative Study of Treatment Outcomes Then and Now." *Hospital and Community Psychiatry* 45, no. 10 (October 1994).

Evenson, Richard C., Richard A. Holland, and Mary E. Johnson. "A Psychiatric Hospital 100 Years Ago, Part II: Patients, Treatment, and Daily Life." *Hospital and Community Psychiatry* 45, no. 10 (October 1994).

Everman, David B., and Alan Stoudemire. "Bipolar Disorder Associated with Klinefelter's Syndrome and Other Chromosomal Abnormalities." *Psychosomatics* 35, no. 1 (Jan/Feb 1994).

Fidler, Donald C. "Helping Our Students Feel How Mental Illness Impacts Lives." *Archives of General Psychiatry.* 19, no. 3 (April 1995).

Fox, Herbert A. "Patients' Fear of and Objection to Electroconvulsive Therapy." *Hospital and Community Psychiatry* 44, no. 4 (April 1993).

Ghadirian, Abdu'l-Missagh, and Normand Roux, "Prevalence and Symptoms at Onset of Bipolar Illness Among Adolescent Inpatients." *Psychiatric Services* 46, no. 4 (1995).

Hermann et al., "Variation in ECT Use in the United States." *American Journal of Psychiatry* 152, no. 6 (June 1995).

Janis, Pam. "A leading expert on manic depression reveals how she overcame its demons." *The Detroit News,* Oct. 6, 1995.

Jefferson, James W., and John H. Greist. "Mood Disorders." *Textbook of Psychiatry*, 2nd edition. Washington, D.C.: American Psychiatric Press, 1994.

Keck, Paul E., Susan L. McElroy, and Charles B. Nemeroff "Anticonvulsants in the Treatment of Bipolar Disorder." *The Journal of Neuropsychiatry and Clinical Neurosciences* 4 (Fall 1992).

Lamb, Richard H. "A Century and a Half of Psychiatric Rehabilitation in the United States." *Hospital and Community Psychiatry* 45, no. 10 (October 1994).

Leibenluft, Ellen. "Women with Bipolar Illness: Clinical and Research Issues." *American Journal of Psychiatry* 153, no. 2 (February 1996).

Nathan, Kalpana I., Dominique L. Musselman, Alan F. Schatzberg, and Charles B. Nemeroff. "Biology of Mood Disorders." *Textbook of Psychopharmacology.*

Washington, D.C.: American Psychiatric Press, 1995.

Pazzaglia, Peggy J., and Robert M. Post. "Contingent Tolerance and Reresponse to Carbamazepine: A Case Study in a Patient with Trigeminal Neuralgia and Bipolar Disorder." *Journal of Neuropsychiatry and Clinical Neurosciences* 4 (Winter 1992).

Quen, Jacques M. "Law and Psychiatry in America over the Past 150 Years." *Hospital and Community Psychiatry* 45, no. 10 (October 1994).

Rieder, Ronald O., Charles A. Kaufmann, and James A. Knowles. "Genetics." *Textbook of Psychiatry*, 2nd edition. Washington, D.C.: American Psychiatric Press, 1994.

Siegfried, Tom, and Sue Goetinck. "Miswired Minds." *Dallas Morning News*, 1996.

Simon, Robert I. "The Law and Psychiatry." *Textbook of Psychiatry*, 2nd edition. Washington, D.C.: American Psychiatric Press, 1994.

Simpson, Sylvia G., Susan E. Folstein, Deborah A. Meyers, and J. Raymond DePaulo. "Assessment of Lineality in Bipolar I Linkage Studies." *American Journal of Psychiatry* 149, no. 12 (December 1992).

Strober, Michael, Susan Schmidt-Lackner, Roberta Freeman, Stacy Bower, Carlyn Lambert, and Mark DeAntonio. "Recovery and Relapse in Adolescents with Bipolar Affective Illness: A Five-Year Naturalistic, Prospective Follow-up." *Journal of the American Academy of Child and Adolescent Psychiatry* 34, no. 6 (June 1995).

Thompson, James W. "Trends in the Development of Psychiatric Services, 1844-1994." *Hospital and Community Psychiatry* 45, no. 10 (October 1994).

Toufexis, Anastasia. "Sliding Past Saturn: A World Authority on Manic Depression Reveals a 30-year Struggle with the Illness." *Time Magazine* 146, no. 11 (September 1995).

Wartik, Nancy. "Missed Diagnosis: Why Depression Goes Untreated in Women." *American Health for Women*, June 1997.

Weiner, Richard D. "Electroconvulsive Therapy." *Treatment of Psychological Disorders*, 2nd edition. 2 vols. Washington, D.C.: American Psychiatric Press, 1995.

Weller, Elizabeth B., Ronald A. Weller, and Mary A. Fristad. "Bipolar Disorder in Children: Misdiagnosis, Underdiagnosis, and Future Directions." *Journal of the American Academy of Child and Adolescent Psychiatry* 34, no. 6 (June 1995).

Wolk, Susan I., and Myrna M. Weissman. "Women and Depression: An Update." *Review of Psychiatry*, vol. 15. Washington, D.C.: American Psychiatric Press, 1995.

APPENDIX

FURTHER READING

American Psychiatric Association. *Diagnostic and Statistical Manual of Mental Disorders*, 4th edition. Washington, D.C.: American Psychiatric Press, 1994.

———. *DSM-IV Sourcebook*, 3 vols. Washington, D.C.: American Psychiatric Press, 1996.

———. *Manual of Clinical Psychopharmacology*, 2nd edition. Washington, D.C.: American Psychiatric Press, 1991.

———. *Textbook of Neuropsychiatry*, 2nd edition. Washington, D.C.: American Psychiatric Press, 1992.

———. *Textbook of Psychiatry*, 2nd edition. Washington, D.C.: American Psychiatric Press, 1994.

———. *Textbook of Psychopharmacology*. Washington, D.C.: American Psychiatric Press, 1995.

———. *Treatment of Psychiatric Disorders*, 2nd edition. 2 vols. Washington, D.C.: American Psychiatric Press, 1995.

Thomas, Clayton C., ed. *Taber's Cyclopedic Medical Dictionary*, 15th edition. Philadelphia: A. Davis Company, 1985.

APPENDIX

GLOSSARY

Affective diseases: Also known as emotional disorders, these diseases relate to human emotions and their influence on behavior.

Bipolar disorder: A type of disorder involving opposing characteristics, such as manic depression, in which the person's moods change from euphoric highs to depressed lows.

Catatonic: A state resembling or caused by schizophrenia, characterized by any or all of the following: physical disturbances of the body, the inability of the body to move, purposeless excitement, and stupor.

Cyclothymic disorder: A type of bipolar disorder characterized by both hypomanic and depressive symptoms that alternate over a lengthy period of time. However, the symptoms are less severe than in other bipolar disorders.

Degeneration: Becoming worse or steadily declining.

Delusional: False beliefs regarding the self, or false perception of events occurring in a person's life.

Depression: The state of feeling sad. In manic depressives, this feeling can be so strong that it can cause inactivity, difficulty in thinking or concentrating, a significant increase or decrease in eating and sleeping habits, feelings of hopelessness, and even suicidal tendencies.

Electroconvulsive therapy (ECT): A treatment for manic depression in which an electric current is sent through an unconscious, medicated patient's brain.

Euphoria: A feeling of elation or well-being.

Euthymia: A feeling of joy or peace of mind, occurring after a major depressive episode, that can last for several days.

Hereditary: A characteristic or quality genetically transmitted from parent to offspring. Manic depression is believed to be hereditary.

Hypomanic episode: One of the mood episodes that compose bipolar disorder. Mental and physical hyperactivity caused by elevation of mood that may last for several weeks or months. A hypomanic episode is less severe than a manic episode.

Lithium: A drug used to treat manic depressive patients. When given in the proper doses, lithium can help relieve symptoms of the disease.

Major depressive episode: One of the mood episodes that compose bipolar disorder. A state of deep depression that may last from two weeks to six months or longer if untreated.

Mania: Heightened and unexplainable excitement or frenzy.

Manic depression: A psychological disorder that is marked by periods of elevated moods (mania) and depression. The disorder is usually diagnosed when a person is a young adult. (See bipolar disorder.)

Manic episode: One of the mood episodes that compose bipolar disorder. Disorganized mental and physical hyperactivity caused by elevation of mood that may last for several days or weeks.

Melancholia: A state of severe depression.

Mixed episode: One of the mood episodes that compose bipolar disorder. A state that rapidly fluctuates between major depressive episodes and manic episodes.

Mood disorder: An abnormal mental condition that affects a person's conscious state of mind and their emotions. Mood disorders include bipolar disorder and unipolar disorder (depression).

Rapid cycling: When a person with bipolar disorder undergoes four or more mood episodes in a 12-month period. This occurs in a small percentage of cases.

Schizophrenia: The disintegration of personality that affects feeling, thought, and conduct, and may involve the presence of multiple or opposing personalities.

Sedative: A drug used to help calm nervousness or excitement.

Serotonin: A chemical, found in the blood serum and mucus of mammals, that causes the blood vessels to narrow.

Unipolar disorder: Also known as depressive disorder, this involves only depression and not manic states.

APPENDIX

INDEX

APPENDIX

PICTURE CREDITS

Senior Consulting Editor Carol C. Nadelson, M.D., is president and chief executive officer of the American Psychiatric Press, Inc., staff physician at Cambridge Hospital, and Clinical Professor of Psychiatry at Harvard Medical School. In addition to her work with the American Psychiatric Association, which she served as vice president in 1981-83 and president in 1985-86, Dr. Nadelson has been actively involved in other major psychiatric organizations, including the Group for the Advancement of Psychiatry, the American College of Psychiatrists, the Association for Academic Psychiatry, the American Association of Directors of Psychiatric Residency Training Programs, the American Psychosomatic Society, and the American College of Mental Health Administrators. In addition, she has been a consultant to the Psychiatric Education Branch of the National Institute of Mental Health and has served on the editorial boards of several journals. Doctor Nadelson has received many awards, including the Gold Medal Award for significant and ongoing contributions in the field of psychiatry, the Elizabeth Blackwell Award for contributions to the causes of women in medicine, and the Distinguished Service Award from the American College of Psychiatrists for outstanding achievements and leadership in the field of psychiatry.

Consulting Editor Claire E. Reinburg, M.A., is editorial director of the American Psychiatric Press, Inc., which publishes about 60 new books and six journals a year. She is a graduate of Georgetown University in Washington, D.C., where she earned bachelor of arts and master of arts degrees in English. She is a member of the Council of Biology Editors, the Women's National Book Association, the Society for Scholarly Publishing, and Washington Book Publishers.

Dan Harmon is a freelance editor and writer living in Charleston, South Carolina. He has written several books on humor and history, and has contributed historical and cultural articles to the *New York Times, Music Journal, Nautilus,* and many other periodicals. He is the managing editor of *Sandlapper: The Magazine of South Carolina* and is editor of *The Lawyer's PC newsletter.*